# Making Your Computer
# A Design And Business Partner

*By Lisa Walker and Steve Blount*

North Light Books
Cincinnati, Ohio

94 93 92 91 90          5 4 3 2 1

The permissions on page 159 constitute an extension of this copyright page.

**Library of Congress Cataloging-In-Publication Data**

Blount, Steve
      Making your computer a design and business partner / by Steve
Blount and Lisa Walker.
         p.   cm.
     Includes index.
     ISBN 0-89134-353-9
     1. Microcomputers. 2. Microcomputers--Purchasing.    I. Walker,
Lisa.  II. Title
     QA76.5.B557    1990
     760'.0285'416--dc20                      90-37938
                                          CIP

Produced for North Light Books, an imprint of F&W Publications, 1507 Dana Avenue, Cincinnati, Ohio 45207 by Blount & Walker Visual Communications, Inc., 8771 Larwin Lane, Orlando, Florida 32817.

Edited by: Diana Martin and Mary Cropper
Designed by: Clare Finney
Art assistant: H. Klaus Heesch
Photography by: Nick Lilavois

# Contents

**5  Introduction**

**7  Section I: Realistic Expectations**

**9  Chapter One: Taking A Digital Partner**
Should You Buy A Graphics Computer? • The Sixty-Second
Computer Check • Taking Control Of Your Destiny
• A Tale Of Two Studios • The Creative Benefits

**33  Chapter Two: What The Computer
Can—And Can't—Do**
Picking Up The Pieces • Bits, Bytes, RAM, And ROM
• Hardware Capabilities • Keyboards / Tablets / Scanners
• Printers / Film Recorders • The Heart Of It All: The Software
• Page Layout / Drawing / Painting • Scanning Software
• Color / Retouching • Spreadsheets / Graphing • Business /
Telecommunications

**51  Chapter Three: A New Way Of Working**
A New Way Of Thinking And Working • Changing The Way You
Work • Taking Responsibility For The Technical Details

**59  Chapter Four: Costs, Benefits, And Cautions**
Real Costs, Real Benefits • Real Costs: One Studio's Experience •
Help Where It Hurts The Most: Production • Profit Opportunities
And A Final Warning • Buyer Beware: Tales From The Dark Side

**71  Section II: What Should I Buy?**

**73  Chapter Five:
How To Buy—Research And Reading**
Getting The Straight Story: You Hear It Through The Grapevine •
Read 'Em And Weep: What The Magazines Don't Tell You •
Manufacturer's (Mis)Information • To Market: Where To Buy

**81  Chapter Six: Hardware Wars**
Hardware Wars: Apple vs. IBM • The IBM Blues • PC To Mac
And Back • The Mac Attacked: New Technologies On The Horizon
• Intangibles: It Just Feels Right

**91  Chapter Seven: Building A Shopping List**
A Computer On Every Desk? • Which Jobs Should You Automate
First? • Shopping For Systems: Forewarned Is Forearmed
• CPUs And The Need For Speed • All In The Family: A Plenitude
Of Peripherals • Printers, Scanners, And RAM • Software Selector
• Pulling Together The Pieces • Penny-Pinching Production

**107  Chapter Eight:
Ante Up—How To Pay The Piper**
Leases And Loans • Insurance

**111  Section III:**
**Making It All Pay Off**

**113  Chapter Nine:**
**Integrating People And Processes**
Integrating Your Computer: Possibilities And Procedures •
Procedure Check • Hornall Anderson Design Works • Glasgow &
Associates • Ziff-Davis Publishing Company • Blount & Walker
Visual Communications • Future Studio: Mark Crumpacker

**121  Chapter Ten: The Well-Trained Studio**
Up The Learning Curve • Training Aids: SIGs, Help Lines,
And Videotapes

**125  Chapter Eleven:**
**Working With A Service Bureau**
Pick Your Partners—Carefully • Test Your Service Bureau • You've
Got A Friend: Upgrading Services

**131  Chapter Twelve:**
**Managing A Computer System**
Keeping It All Together—And Working • Software Compatibility And
Power Solutions • Well-Furnished Workstations: Are Ergonomics
Necessary?

**137  Chapter Thirteen:**
**Things That Can—And Will—Go Wrong**
Common Problems: A Few Of Our Least Favorite Things
• Viral Infections: Causes, Cures

**141  Chapter Fourteen: Business Class**
Business Class: Software For A Smart Studio • Estimating, Tracking,
Accounting • Studio/Soft: Dreams For Design Studio Management

**147  Chapter Fifteen: Heading For A Far Horizon**
Changing Times

**151  Chapter Sixteen: Reference And Resources**
What Is PostScript? • Color From The Desktop • Rasters And
Resolution • Resource Listings

**159  Index**

Three years ago, we found ourselves sitting in a room surrounded by a small mountain of boxes. We had just spent $16,000 on a graphics computer designed to do things we already knew how to do perfectly well with a knife, a T-square, and a hand waxer (total cost, $90).

We'd gleefully blown our capital budget for the next six months in one fell swoop, but we were happy. Here's why: We'd just finished a book project that consumed three months of paste-up time and $6,000 worth of photostats. We had the chance to expand our business dramatically by producing more books, but the expense of type, stats, and paste-up labor was destroying our budgets.

After months of research and a lot of soul searching, we concluded that the only profitable answer to our dilemma was to buy and learn to operate a desktop publishing system.

Using it, in the past few years we've designed and produced books containing more than 2,500 pages and 4,200 color illustrations. We've spent almost nothing on photostats, our type costs average less than half of what they were on that first project, and there is no paste-up.

Sound too good to be true? We thought so, too. At the outset, that's what worried us. If all of these benefits were real, why didn't everyone already have graphics computers?

The months just before and just after we took the plunge were the most confusing and anxiety-ridden in our studio's existence.

We felt we had to buy a graphic arts computer to stay competitive, but what if it didn't work the way the manufacturers claimed? What if it wouldn't actually cut our paste-up time dramatically? What if the equipment cost more than it saved in supplies and labor? What if the quality of the type that came from the computer wasn't acceptable?

This is the book we wish we'd had—a survival guide for that critical first six months.

Drawing on our own experiences and those of dozens of graphic studios that have installed computers, we've organized the book around the three big questions you need to answer:

"Should I buy a computer system?"

"If so, what pieces should I buy, how do I decide what brands are best, and how do I finance it?"

"And third, once I have a computer, how can I manage my studio—the people, the equipment, the physical space—to get the maximum possible benefit?"

We'll try to help you avoid the many booby traps that await the adventurous: Poorly-written software manuals, the less-than-rigorous product reviews given graphic arts equipment in the computer press, the inexpert advice offered by too many computer dealers, the danger of convincing yourself that you must have one of the many really neat (translate "expensive") toys when something less impressive (and less costly) will do the job.

No matter what the ads say, graphics computers are not one-size-fits-all, so we've interviewed designers from many different kinds of studios and have developed a series of worksheets to help you determine whether you need a computer and, if so, what kind.

We've looked at the business side of design, too, asking designers how they've used computers to improve the efficiency of their studios and increase profits.

The last section of the book contains reference material and names and addresses for manufacturers, users groups, and more.

But the first question you should ask about buying a graphics computer is the most basic:

"Why should I?"

That's the subject of Chapter One.

# Section I:
# Realistic Expectations

**9** Chapter One:
**Taking A Digital Partner**

**33** Chapter Two: What The Computer
**Can—And Can't—Do**

**51** Chapter Three:
**A New Way Of Working**

**59** Chapter Four:
**Costs, Benefits, And Cautions**

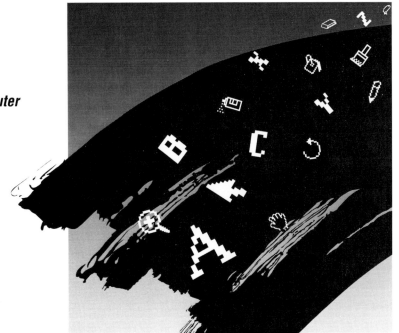

# Chapter One:
# Taking A Digital Partner

**Should You Buy A Graphics Computer?**

**The Sixty-Second Computer Check**

**Taking Control Of Your Destiny**

**A Tale Of Two Studios**

**The Creative Benefits**

## Should You Buy A Graphics Computer?

*"The application of computers to the graphic arts is truly revolutionary. They will have as much impact on the way artists work as did the invention of movable type."*

—Lance Hidy, designer/illustrator, Newburyport, Massachusetts

If Lance Hidy's assessment makes you a little nervous, you're not alone. After all, if you really liked computers, you'd have become a computer programmer instead of an artist, right? However you feel about being chained to a whirring beige box festooned with flashing lights and sprouting clumps of tentacle-like cables, deciding whether or not to add computers to your design practice is the single most important business decision you will make.

The graphic arts have arrived at a watershed. Choosing to use—or not use—computer-based design and production equipment will have the most profound effect imaginable on how much revenue you can generate, how much profit you make, how your studio is organized, your choices in personnel, and even what kinds of tasks you do from hour to hour.

However ominous that sounds, fortunately, the news from the front is mostly good.

### Power For The People

In the interviews we conducted in the course of writing this book, we didn't find one studio that, having installed a graphics computer, removed it and went back to manual design and production.

The reason for that will be obvious after you've produced your first large, complicated project on a graphics computer. Some years ago, H.L. Mencken observed that, "The power of the press belongs to the man who owns one." A computer graphics system can put the capabilities—and the power—afforded by typesetting equipment, photostat cameras, and a large paste-up staff on the top of your desk.

This does four things for you: It allows you to experiment freely, quickly, and conveniently with illustration styles, headline treatments, type styles, even color schemes. Second, it puts control of the design process—its timing, pace, and quality—in your hands and takes it away from the outside typesetters and others who often dictate your schedule. Third, it reduces the amount of time and energy expended coordinating the work of people both inside and outside of your studio. Last, and hardly least important, it can reduce costs and increase your profits.

In our case, the time we once spent orchestrating the efforts of six people in three different firms is now spent designing. That means more productive hours per day and more revenues at the end of the month. It also means fewer checks to write and more profit. There is a temptation to automate steps that are faster and cheaper to do by hand. But, uniformly, the experiences of other studios reflects our experience: Using graphics computers results in higher productivity and lower costs.

This is the power, revolutionary in its scope, that Lance Hidy and many other designers have found inside that whirring beige box. Instead of thinking of the computer as an adversary, they have come to see it as a design and business partner, one that can increase their productivity and make their studios more profitable.

### The Disclaimer

This is the point in automobile advertising where they say: "Your actual mileage may vary."

In fact, a computer is of no value unless you know what you will use it for.

Most designers buy a computer for specific jobs, such as illustration or laying out pages. Six months later, many find they're using it for much of their daily work. Some also say computers help them to be better businesspersons.

Some of the more obvious tasks that designers find are accomplished with more ease or cost-effectiveness on a computer include:

Development of logotypes

Illustration

Typesetting

Volume mechanical production

Design and production of catalogs, books, magazines, and newsletters

Creating advertisements

Marketing presentations

Producing design comps

Presentation slides/transparencies

Masks for screen printing

The *range* of things that can be done on relatively inexpensive graphics computers is staggering: make color separations, create multimedia presentations, create whole new kinds of communications in the form of videotex and hypermedia, create and edit soundtracks for presentations or videotapes, and store illustrations in graphic databases.

The key to reaping the maximum benefit of a graphics computer is to integrate it into your studio's daily workflow, rather than just hanging it on the back end of the process as an afterthought.

This doesn't mean that you must (or even should) go from an art table to a monitor overnight. Or that you should browbeat reluctant associates into immediately giving up their masking fluid for a mouse.

Many of the designers we spoke with in the course of writing this book slowly worked up to full integration of graphics computers with traditional methods; many are still in the process of making the adjustment.

There are as many different models of how to go about adding a graphics computer to a studio as there are studios. It's possible to gain some of the advantages—especially in reducing the cost of outside type and photostats—by bringing in one workstation and using it as a photostat and type terminal. One person can feed a number of other designers with galley type and positioning images to be used on traditional mechanicals.

This may be a place to start. It will give you a chance to live with the computer for a while before you make a major financial commitment to the hardware and an irreversible commitment to revising the way your studio works.

Whether you ultimately decide to buy a graphics computer now or to pass, whether you buy several workstations or one, the key to keeping your financial risk at a minimum and your frustration level from outstripping your patience is to think the process through. This book is designed to help you do that.

## Whose Life Is This, Anyway?

Computers are insidious. Just when you think you've got them cornered—got their place in the natural order of things all figured out—they surprise you. They grow more tentacles. They suddenly become indispensable in yet another area of your life. For years, there was a clear, well-understood distinction between Macintosh and IBM computers, for example. IBM was for business and the Macintosh was for drawing pictures. Accounting? Forget it. Database management? A pipe dream.

Although few designers use them, IBM-compatible desktop computers can be a useful graphic arts tool, especially for Computer Aided Design (CAD), manipulating three-dimensional images, and combining video with computer-generated art. The Macintosh, meanwhile, has grown into a suit and tie. There are a number of suitably powerful programs for managing numbers, data, and cash flow that run on the Macintosh today.

Machines that had a defined place in the business universe have expanded, outgrowing our notions of how to best use, or not use, them.

For designers, there are two dangers in the computer's tendency to keep going beyond the comfortable (and correct) niches we carve for them in our minds. The first is that the technology will pass us by while we're not looking; that someone else will get a technological edge that will damage our business. Unfortunately, it does happen.

The second danger is that, in a rush to keep from being passed by, we will be stampeded into making unnecessary purchases, or worse yet, will abandon traditional processes that prove to be more effective or more cost-efficient in the long run. This happens too.

It's your life and the studio is your business. It belongs to you, not to a machine. However, computer technology in the graphic arts field is a reality, a rising wave that can buoy your work and your profits, or swamp you and dash you down onto the rocky shores of obsolescence. If you're a fan of Oriental philosophy, you might say that the way to meet this challenge is to take control of your own destiny: Meet the computer on its own turf, understand its strengths and weaknesses, and decide if you need one from a position of knowledge rather than fear. If, on the other hand, you're a fan of the Green Bay Packers, you could just say that the best defense is a good offense.

Whether your reaction is Oriental or Occidental, don't let it be *accidental*; don't let your clients and suppliers determine how your studio will fare over the next few years because you failed to make the decisions for yourself.

## Ballad Of A Hired Gun

It may help if you think of a graphics computer as just another employee. Granted, you can't buy or sell employees (though there are some service firms who will hire your employees and then lease them back to you).

On many other counts, however, graphics computers are like ordinary employees. When you buy a computer, you're really hiring it (hopefully with a defined purpose in mind).

The questions you need to ask beforehand are pretty similar to those you'd consider before hiring a human: What will this employee do? How will they contribute to the success of the studio and to your quality of life? What skills will they need to be successful? What should their resumé (in this case, the specifications sheet) include? How will you manage them for optimum benefit? How can you get them to fit into your studio without making everyone else uncomfortable? Will the studio's procedures have to be changed to make the most of this new employee's abilities? Where will they sit? Who'll be their boss? What kinds of supplies and support systems will they need?

There's one other area of similarity, too: References. You need to talk to people who've employed computers. What was their experience? What kind of work has the computer done for them?

## Information Please

Until recently, getting this information hasn't been easy. Affordable graphics computer systems capable of producing reproduction-quality art have only been available since 1984. It wasn't until 1986 that the equipment that allowed these computers to use a traditional phototypesetter as a printing device became widely available. Compared to the length of experience designers have had with brushes, paints, even technical pens and airbrushes, that's literally the blink of an eye.

This means you'll have to do some digging. There are magazines to read: Read them. There are designers—probably several in your own community—who already have graphics computers: Visit them. There are manufacturers who make computers and software programs for designers: Call them.

If you picked up this book, you've probably already started asking the questions and doing the research. Even if you understand only half of what you've seen, take heart. It isn't a reflection on your intelligence. Computer journals and the more technically minded among us tend to lapse into jargon. Jargon does serve a useful purpose; it's a kind of verbal shorthand that speeds up communication about complex subjects. For the experienced computer user, this is a good thing. If you're on the outside looking in, however, it sounds like so much Swahili and is just about as informative. We'll try to explain some of the jargon as we go and keep its use to a minimum.

We believe that the best people to talk to about graphics computers aren't manufacturers, retailers, or engineers, but rather the graphic artists who use them.

## A Tale Of Two Studios

### IMAGEMARC: Automation For The One-Man Band

*Marc Passarelli*
*Founded 1987*
*One designer*
*Computer graphics equipment: Macintosh SE, Apple Laserwriter IINT, extended keyboard, 65-megabyte hard disk drive, 2.5 megabytes RAM*

When Princeton, New Jersey, designer Marc Passarelli saw a Macintosh computer demonstrated, he knew immediately that it could have a major effect on his business. He bought the equipment at a cost of $10,000. Three years later, Passarelli has doubled his revenues and doesn't question the decision to buy a computer for his one-man studio.

"Every time I bill a job, I lick the stamp, put it on the envelope, and say 'God, I'm glad I bought a Mac.' The margin between success and failure in this business is pretty small. I'm not getting Fortune 500 clients yet, but I am making a profit. The Mac really contributes to that. I can take a project from rough sketch to finished film right on the screen. When I bill a job, I feel the computer helped me get through all of the steps it took to earn my fee.

"My first exposure to graphics computers came when I attended a Mac Expo. I saw computers as a way to save money on typesetting—in fact, my type bills have dropped 30 percent—and to eliminate paste up from galleys. I also felt a system would save time on comps; I wouldn't have to trace letters from type catalogs.

"I bought a Macintosh Plus and an Imagewriter printer. They were decent tools, but weren't capable of professional results, so I moved up to a Macintosh SE a year later.

"Most of my work doesn't involve long galleys. I can bang out the type on the Mac and have control over the entire product. One of the biggest advantages is that I don't have to send out for type corrections. Sometimes when you spec type, you imagine it one way, and when it's set, it just doesn't look like you thought it would. It's very difficult to visualize what some faces will look like after they've been condensed or expanded. With the Mac, I can modify the type right on the screen, print it out immediately, and take a look. It's like being able to look over your typesetter's shoulder all day, except you're running the show. How many typesetters will let you come in and watch them work? None. You don't see your work until it comes out on RC paper. If it isn't right, you have to pay for corrections.

"About 80 percent of my work is done on the computer. I still sketch concepts and use markers, paste the repro sheets to a mechanical, and mark the printer's instructions on an overlay. But recently I've gone right from laser proofs to plate-ready film on a few jobs.

"My advice to other graphic designers who are thinking about adding computers to their studio is, 'Don't think twice. If you have the financial means to buy a system, get it. You won't regret it.'"

*Hans Flink*
*Founded 1972; Seven designers*
*Computer graphics equipment: Macintosh II,*
*Apple Laserwriter IINT, extended keyboard,*
*60-megabyte disk drive, 2 megabytes RAM,*
*Viking 19-inch monitor, Mitsubishi scanner*

Designer Hans Flink has been a major player in the ultra-competitive packaging design scene in New York since 1972. His client list is enviable, including Richardson-Vicks and Chesebrough-Ponds, just to name Fortune 500 accounts. Despite the torrent of advertising loosed by computer manufacturers, Flink didn't buy a graphics computer until 1988.

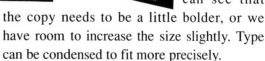

"I began hearing so much about other design studios using graphics computers, I felt at a loss because I wasn't one of them. Now that I have a computer, I feel more informed. I know what other designers are talking about and what they're doing.

"In reality, of course, the music isn't in the piano, it's in the piano player. There are many young designers right out of school who are comfortable using a graphics computer, but they haven't had enough design experience to do really great work. This whole area of computer-aided design will improve vastly when experienced designers are computer literate.

"The computer is a good tool, but it isn't the right tool for every task. We ask ourselves, 'Could we do this well on the computer?' For instance, we don't use it to generate initial ideas. A sketch pad is better for that.

With a pad, you can jump from idea to idea in seconds. With a computer, you can generate a lot of variations in a short time, but all of them will be in the same realm; it takes several minutes to scan in elements for a different approach.

"Once the rough idea is formed, the computer is terrific. It's mind-boggling how quickly it can work. We're currently designing the back label of a coffee can. The type has to flow around a photograph. The computer can do that instantaneously. Where once we would have sent the type to a typesetter, waited until the next day, made corrections, and then waited again, now we can see the results on the screen immediately. We can see that the copy needs to be a little bolder, or we have room to increase the size slightly. Type can be condensed to fit more precisely.

"But the real payoff comes during the final stages of production. If the client wants to change a word, we can do it quickly and save our clients money as well. We're also able to create elements—such as radius curves—with great precision. It's a real chore to draw a line frame with a radius corner using a technical pen and a compass.

"Ultimately, I think much of the pre-press work will be done on computers. That will give designers control right into the plate-making stage, and we'll avoid having color separators make design decisions."

## The Creative Benefits

So much time is spent talking up the cost benefits of using a graphics computer that the very considerable creative benefits are often overlooked. All of this talk about making things cheaper leads some artists to assume that they'll have to give up the control and quality they get by working with galleys of type, a T-square, and a knife.

Our experience points in just the opposite direction.

*Computers expand the amount of time you can devote to the creative aspects of design* by making the production of camera-ready mechanical art simpler, faster, and cheaper.

*They make your design time more productive* by allowing you to quickly explore different looks, changing type and graphics as fast as you can point-and-click with a mouse, stylus, or keyboard. The results can be viewed on the screen or printed on a laser printer immediately.

*Multiple permutations of illustrations and logos can be generated automatically.* This is done by a process called "tweening," originally developed for animators. You input two shapes, say the letter "B" and a butterfly. The computer then generates a series of illustrations in which the outline of the letter gradually changes to that of the butterfly. Adobe Illustrator®, a popular software program, has a tweening feature.

*Shapes, colors, and textures can be generated and viewed on-screen with minimal effort.* Dropping colored text onto a background of colored triangles (or any other texture or pattern) can be done in a matter of two to five minutes and viewed or printed immediately. Most drawing programs come with a library of several dozen texture patterns and allow you to modify or create new ones by simply clicking on a checkerboard-style matrix with the mouse.

*A good rough—complete with correct typestyles, halftones, and even color type and images—can be created very quickly and printed out immediately.* Many designers say these roughs look almost as good as the comps they used to produce manually.

*These roughs can be turned into presentation-grade comps very quickly* by adding color photocopies in the image areas and some colored overlays. Or, if you have a service bureau that has a color scanner and printer, full-color comps can be printed directly from your electronic files. Better, more complete comps translates into more effective communication with your clients, and, some designers say, into an easier "sale" of design concepts. This can speed up approvals, pushing work through the studio faster. It can also allow you to spend more time on the creative aspects of the business and less time holding the client's hand, talking him through something that's a bit hard to visualize.

*Because the commands that created the roughs are stored electronically, they can be used as the basis for the final mechanical art.* This eliminates much of the duplication of time that occurs when manually translating roughs into mechanicals. There is no mechanical board to rule up, for example. You will spend some time fine-tuning the electronic file. But once that tuning is done, it is ready to be sent to an imagesetter and output photographically as final mechanical art (on RC paper) or as film negatives, ready to be stripped and plated.

*In production-intensive work, one designer can create a template for others to follow,* bringing consistency to a large project without the need for constant supervision by the chief designer.

At one firm with a large volume of annual reports, senior designers create six to eight pages of typical layouts for each report in an electronic file. Layout artists use these files as "templates," placing text and pictures in them to complete the layouts for the reports.

*Anything that can be scanned in—photos, tracings, line drawings, even three-dimensional objects—can be used as the basis for illustrations.* A wide variety of airbrush and pen-like effects can be applied to the illustrations, which can be output at reproduction quality at any size or placed into page layout files.

To create "Temple" (above) illustrator Lance Hidy used a Macintosh II computer to collage a variety of images taken from 35mm transparencies. Instead of using a knife and paste, the pieces were seamlessly assembled in an electronic file. The slides were scanned on a Nikon LS-3500 scanner. Hidy then combined and retouched the images using Adobe PhotoShop software. The color separations were made on a Macintosh using PhotoShop and composite film made by Sanjay Sakhuja of Digital Prepress in San Francisco. "Temple" was printed by Carl Sesto, of Pressroom Gallery in Newburyport, Massachusetts. © 1989 Lance Hidy.

These headlines were specified to fit the cover illustration, which is by McRay Magelby. Designing justified headlines is made much easier by the computer's ability to condense and track type on-screen.

A full range of PostScript effects were used for the jacket of The Best New U.S. and International Label Designs 2 *(below)*. The airbrush-like fades are gradient and radial fills created in Adobe Illustrator. They were supplied as positives on RC paper, rather than as pre-separated film negatives.

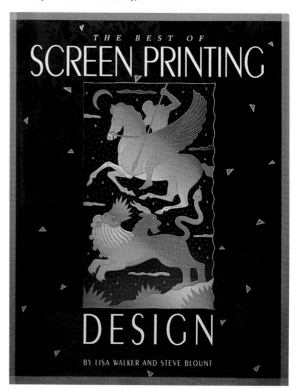

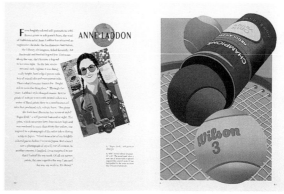

For us, the computer functions as a design tool and production tool simultaneously. Designing complex wraparounds such as those shown in the spread above *(*The Best of Screen Printing Designs*)* or at left *(*Designs For Marketing No. 1: Primo Angeli*)* would be difficult without knowing how the text will fit. Using the computer, we can see the wrap on screen and edit the copy to fit. When the design is finished, the spread is a camera-ready mechanical.

Created in Micrografx Designer on an IBM-compatible computer, this piece is a case study in the use of time-saving illustration techniques. The bottom figure, of course, is a mirror image of the top figure, which has been duplicated and turned upside down. The placard that carries the "M," the type, and the spade symbol have also been duplicated. Notice how the illustrator used the placards and a gradated ribbon to cover the seam where the pieces were joined. The card itself was duplicated several times. The copies were rotated clockwise slightly to produce the card "deck" and each succeeding card was given a slightly darker tint of black. © 1989 Micrografx, Inc.

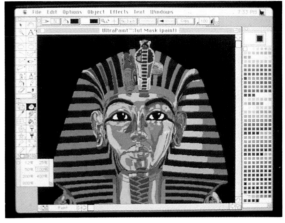

An image under construction in Ultra Paint shows how works in progress look to a computer artist. Instead of a canvas, rack of brushes, and a palette, the computer displays a "tool box" (the strip at left containing tools such as the "pencil," "brush," and "eraser") and a color selection chart. © 1990 Deneba Systems, Inc.

This screen dump from TypeStyler shows how the program conforms type to an arbitrary baseline. Font manipulation programs, like TypeStyler, are very useful in creating logos, symbols, and signs. © 1990 Broderbund Software.

Contrasted with the hard-edged style favored by many computer artists, "Dancers II" (right) illustrates how malleable the graphics computer really is. Artist Steve Lyons used PixelPaint to create a flowing, impressionistic piece that reminds the viewer more of tapestry than of photography. © 1990 SuperMac Technology.

*The ability to pick up and move design elements from piece to piece is especially useful for corporate identity programs. The client's identity, whether a mark alone or a mark combined with type, can be stored electronically as an Encapsulated PostScript File or other graphic and called up for use in an electronic document at any time. When making repetitive mechanicals, such as those for the stationery program on the opposite page, the time saved can be considerable. Brochure by Pat Davis Design.*

Mechanical art for PostScript effects, such as the subtle blue fade used on this letterhead and brochure, can be created relatively quickly. Better yet, just as a logotype can be held "on file" on a computer hard disk, so can these effects. Rather than having to airbrush a new mask for each piece, the designer can call up the fade and rescale it to the proper size. The effects can also be called up and used for other projects. Many designers keep a "library" of such effects on their disk drives. Design by Pat Davis Design.

21

Informational graphics can be created quickly using a spreadsheet program.
This chart was created using WingZ software. The separation was made
directly from a thermal wax image printed on a Tektronix 4693D color laser
printer. Because the 4693D printer doesn't have a PostScript language interpreter, the text looks jagged. A laser printer with a PostScript
interpreter would render the text smoothly. Overhead
transparencies could be made from this file
very easily by simply printing on
acetate instead of paper.
© 1989 Informix Software, Inc.

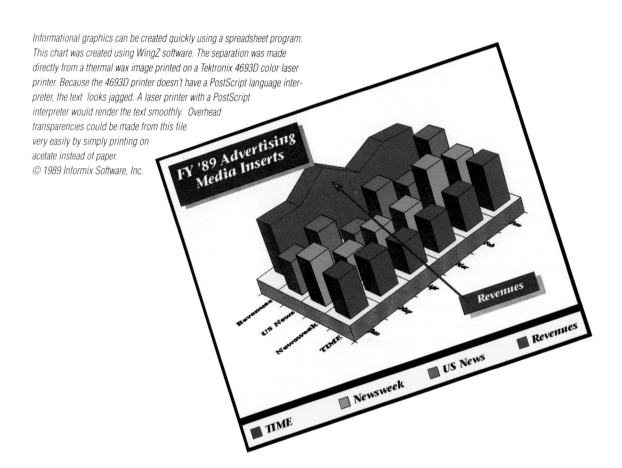

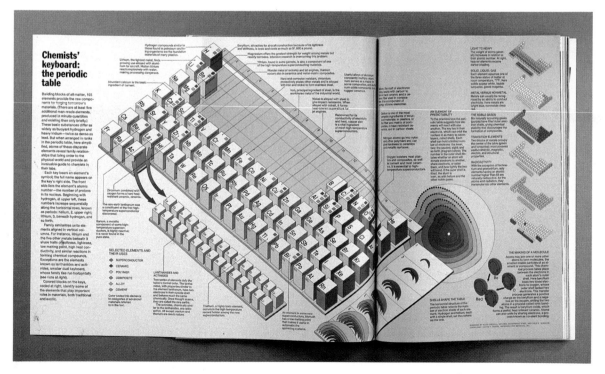

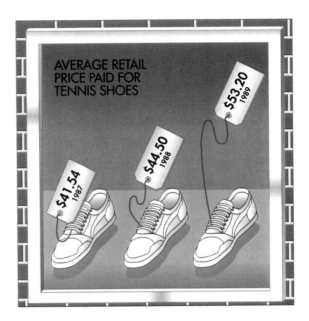

Dale Glasgow created the diagrams for Hurlers (below) and "Chemists' Keyboard" (opposite page, bottom) using Aldus FreeHand. The repeating elements in Hurlers —the fingers, the baseball, the diamond, the pitcher, and batter—were drawn once, then duplicated and repositioned as needed. The ability to duplicate images makes it possible for Glasgow to "mass produce" a series of illustrations quickly without having to start from scratch for each new piece. Also, because the main elements used in the various illustrations are duplicates, there is a sense of unity and uniformity that would have been hard to achieve if the images had been rendered by hand. Rather than use a word count and leaving space for the text of the illustrations, Glasgow started with the edited text, specified it in the correct size and face in the Macintosh, and designed the illustrations around the text. This eliminates the need to resepecify text or alter an illustration later if the space left for words is inadequate. Hurlers © 1989, Redefinitions. "Chemists' Keyboard" also makes use of repeating shapes, such as the shells of the atoms in the lower right and the "keys" themselves. © 1989, National Geographic Society.

Created in Aldus FreeHand by illustrator Dale Glasgow, the chart above was printed on a DuPont 4Cast sublimal dye digital proof printer. The separation was made directly from the dye print. Glasgow can supply his work as an electronic disk file, film negatives, or as a dye proof. The work could also be output to a film recorder to make slides, or to a color laser printer. This flexibility of output can't be achieved when working conventionally. Multiple copies in different media can be made easily and the illustrator can keep a copy of the original file for himself. © 1989, Glasgow & Associates.

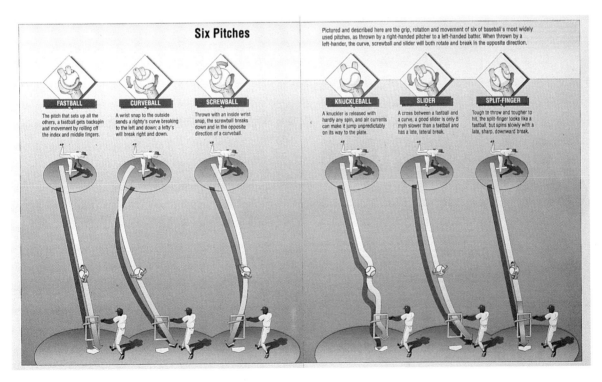

**Six Pitches**

Pictured and described here are the grip, rotation and movement of six of baseball's most widely used pitches, as thrown by a right-handed pitcher to a left-handed batter. When thrown by a left-hander, the curve, screwball and slider will both rotate and break in the opposite direction.

**FASTBALL**
The pitch that sets up all the others, a fastball gets backspin and movement by rolling off the index and middle fingers.

**CURVEBALL**
A wrist snap to the outside sends a righty's curve breaking to the left and down; a lefty's will break right and down.

**SCREWBALL**
Thrown with an inside wrist snap, the screwball breaks down and in the opposite direction of a curveball.

**KNUCKLEBALL**
A knuckler is released with hardly any spin, and air currents can make it jump unpredictably on its way to the plate.

**SLIDER**
A cross between a fastball and a curve, a good slider is only 5 mph slower than a fastball and has a late, lateral break.

**SPLIT-FINGER**
Tough to throw and tougher to hit, the split-finger looks like a fastball, but spins slowly with a late, sharp, downward break.

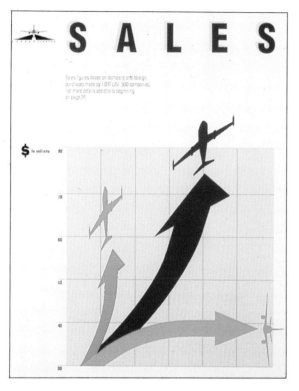

Left: Complete type, illustrations, and even color separations can be handled directly from the keyboard for simple sales pieces, such as the one at left, created in Adobe Illustrator. If you have clip art on file, it's possible to do a piece like this without getting up from your desk or waiting for type or stats. © 1989 Adobe Systems, Inc.

Below: Complex modeling and shading take a while for most illustrators to master. Once learned, the techniques can be used almost—but not quite—as one would use an airbrush. The F-16 is by David Haber and was created in Micrografx Designer. © 1990 Micrografx, Inc.

Right: The Howtek Pixel Master inkjet printer used to print the image at right created a rough, highly-textured surface. The texture may be appropriate for some subjects, and inkjet printers generally cost less than thermal wax or dye sublimation printers. The illustration was created in Canvas by David Rumfelt. © 1990 Deneba Systems, Inc.

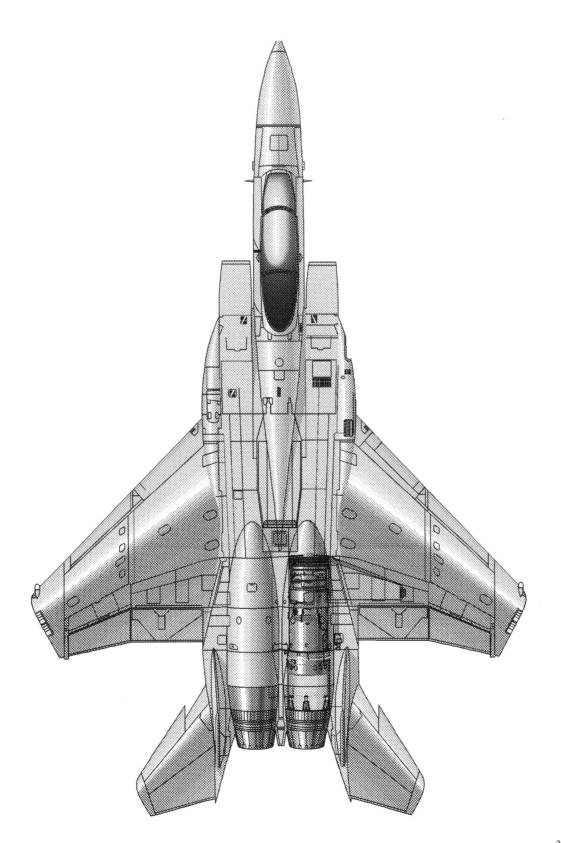

Right: Drawing and painting programs that run on IBM compatible computers have begun to challenge the dominance of the Macintosh in the area of color illustration. Created in Micrografx Designer, this poster makes good use of repeating patterns, one of the strong suits of graphics computers. © 1989 Micrografx, Inc.

Below: The availability of image scanners and good scanning software make graphics computers a good choice for illustrations that combine photography with hand rendering. "Living Color" (below) was created in PixelPaint by Didier Cremieux. © SuperMac Technology.

Bottom: It may take a while to get used to drawing or painting with a mouse, but as "Skybox" by Ron Cobb shows, once the technique is mastered the results can closely resemble those obtained through photography or the use of oil paints. © SuperMac Technology.

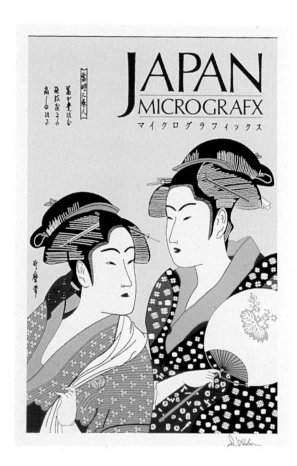

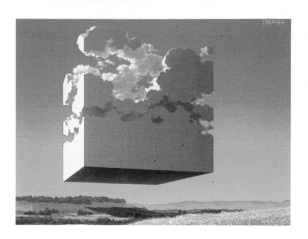

Opposite page, top: This sign for a Korean amusement park was rendered in Pixel Paint Professional by Mark Crumpacker. Three-dimensional shading —difficult at best even for an accomplished airbrush artist—can be created readily using a computer. Some programs even allow you to model the curves of a surface by positioning hidden "light sources." The computer then renders shadows appropriate to that placement. © 1990 Mark Crumpacker.

Opposite page, lower left: Created in Adobe Illustrator, this gumball machine demonstrates how the program handles curves and how it can handle type as a graphic object. The shading on the front and base of the machine was created using Illustrator's blend tool. In this case, the object being blended was the outline of the base of the machine. A very faint banding effect can be distinguished where the blended shapes meet. © 1989, Adobe Systems, Inc.

Opposite page, lower right: Using Micrografx Designer, David Haber created this silkscreen print reminiscent of the broad, flat colors found in Japanese woodblock prints. © 1990 Micrografx, Inc.

Designers say the ability to scale illustrations and type up or down, and to repeat elements or formatted layouts without redrawing them or making photostats is a big plus when working on designs for packaging. The fluid, modern feeling of the illustrations for these videocassette covers shows that the range of effects and styles that can be achieved using a graphics computer is limited more by the designer's imagination than by the quality of the tool. © Pat Davis Design.

Opposite page, top: Aldus Freehand and PageMaker were used together to create this literature pack. The ability to merge graphics with text easily and see the results on the screen immediately is one of the most useful features of graphics computers. © 1989, Aldus Corporation.

Opposite page, bottom: Manually rendering a number of color variations of a single label can be arduous, expensive, and time consuming. Using a graphics computer, changing colors—in this case for different flavors of a mineral water—can be done very quickly. The results can be viewed on a color monitor, imaged on a 35mm slide (as these were), printed on a color printer, or they can be color separated and a color key made. Created in Adobe Illustrator. © 1989 Adobe Systems, Inc.

1

2

3

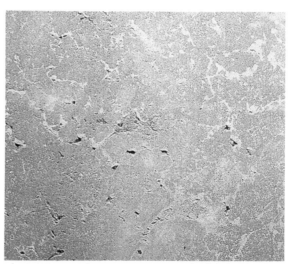

4

5

6

7

This series of slides by designer Mark Crumpacker shows how he builds an image of a proposed new product package in the computer, then places it in a shelf study with competing brands to evaluate how much visual impact it will have in a retail store. Crumpacker used what he calls his "dream worksta-tion"—a fully-loaded Macintosh II , color monitor, color scanner, and film recorder—along with Adobe Illustrator and Pixel Paint Professional to create these images.

1. A technical drawing of the proposed package and label is done in Adobe Illustrator.

2. The Illustrator image is imported into Pixel Paint Professional, and colors and a background are added.

3. A mask is made by filling the white areas of the package with "mask" and then reversing the mask, so that the background will show through.

4. A piece of stone is scanned and its image stored to be used as a textured background.

5. Using the mask created in step 3, the image of the stone is merged with the colored label created in step 2.

6. Shadows, light sources, and reflections are added to give the package a three-dimensional look.

7. The finished package is combined with the scanned images of competing products. The package can now be evaluated, even though no physical comp has been produced. This makes it possible to look at several proposed designs and judge them against existing competitive products without the expense of creating and photographing them.

THE WILBUR AALFS LIBRARY
SIOUX CITY PUBLIC LIBRARY
DEDICATION · 25 FEBRUARY 1990

*From a distance, this Lance Hidy poster for the Aalfs Library appears stylistically similar to some of his pre-Macintosh work. A close examination, however, reveals the subtle influence of technology: The clouds have a pointillistic texture created by the computer and the pixels that make up the tree branches have been exaggerated to give the impression of light filtering through the leaves. Hidy created the poster in Adobe Illustrator. Composite negatives were output using a Scitex film plotter, and the poster was silk screened by Mink Brook Editions. © 1990 Lance Hidy.*

# Chapter Two: What The Computer Can—And Can't—Do

**Picking Up The Pieces**

**Keyboards / Tablets / Scanners**

**Printers / Film Recorders**

**The Heart Of It All: The Software**

**Page Layout / Drawing / Painting**

**Scanning Software**

**Color / Retouching**

**Spreadsheets / Graphing**

**Business / Telecommunications**

## Picking Up The Pieces

Perhaps the scariest part of buying a graphics computer is the uncertainty: Will it do what the salesman claimed? Will it be a cost-effective purchase? Will it terminally disrupt your studio?

There's no easy way to answer these questions with confidence. While you needn't become a tech-head to make an informed purchase (or an informed decision *not* to purchase), you will need a grasp of your studio's needs and of the capabilities of the equipment. You won't get either from the average computer salesman. He doesn't know design and he doesn't know printing. You're going to have to learn a little bit about computers out of *the* most basic motive: Self-preservation.

Fortunately, computers are pretty simple devices as long as you don't have to actually fix one, which you won't. We operate on the "black box" theory: We don't need to know *how* a computer does what it does, we only need to know *what* it will do.

While computers aren't very good at thinking or making judgments (such as what color a headline should be), they're very good at following rules and procedures. With the right instructions, they can be made to calculate the flight trajectory of the space shuttle or draw a perfect set of concentric circles. Those things are all very nice, but the questions you need to answer are: Will a graphics computer make your business more profitable or your work easier? How much will the gear cost? How will it affect your studio? The purpose of this book is to help you analyze whether the things you're likely to use a graphics computer for make it cost-effective.

First, what is a graphics computer? You need to know a little bit about the various pieces of hardware before you'll be able to make an informed choice—whether to buy, what to buy, how much to spend, and what to expect of the equipment after it's installed.

### The Components

A computer is composed of a number of different parts. Unlike the early Apple Macintosh, in which all of the pieces were integrated into a single cabinet, most computers (including the later Macintosh models) are built like component stereo systems. The machine that does the thinking is called the CPU (Central Processing Unit). This is the box that contains the circuit boards and plays host to the other pieces, which are called peripherals. CPU is also sometimes used to refer to the specific silicon chip that directs traffic inside the computer, calling up data from memory and sending it to another chip to be altered.

Getting the right assortment of peripherals is essential to reaping the full benefits of a graphics computer.

### Keyboards

Your basic tool for interacting with the computer is the keyboard. Don't panic. You won't need to take typing classes in night school to use a graphics computer effectively. When you are designing or drawing—as opposed to typing text—most of the instructions can be entered with a mouse or by typing a few characters, such as a number of picas for the width of a column.

Keyboards are as individual as the manufacturers who make them. It is also possible to customize the key layout of your keyboard, using a software package to assign long strings of commands (such as the commands to open a new page layout file, divide it into three columns, and set the type specs) to a single key or combination of keys. Most IBM-compatible machines are supplied with keyboards that have numerical keypads and function keys (extra keys you can use to store long groups of commands). Macintosh computers aren't. The standard Macintosh keyboard has a numerical keypad, but no function keys. It's worth the extra charge (about $75, depending on your dealer) to get the "extended keyboard." Using function keys can cut layout time significantly and will reduce your frustration level even more, as they can perform complex tasks with a single keystroke.

## The Mouse

The mouse and its sibling, the trackball, are the greatest things since sliced cheese. The mouse is a pointing device that allows you to direct the computer's attention anywhere on the screen. You simply roll the mouse around your desk on

## Bits, Bytes, RAM, And ROM

The first time we heard a computer dealer's spiel, we thought we were listening to a recitation of Hindu deities. There is a connection between computer terms and religion: Salesmen often use the terms as priests have used incantations for eons—to confuse, and thus gain power over, the rest of us. Rule No. 1: Don't be afraid to ask a salesman to explain his statements in plain English. Rule No. 2: Memorize this list:

*Bits:* Bits are the basic units of electronic data. A bit is either one ("on") or zero ("off").

*Bytes:* Like the dots and dashes of Morse Code, bits are grouped together to produce computer "words" that can stand for a letter of the alphabet or a specific instruction. These words are called bytes. There are three classes of graphics computers being sold for desktop use: eight-bit, sixteen-bit, and thirty-two bit machines. An eight-bit machine uses words that are eight bits long; a sixteen-bit machine uses words that are sixteen bits long. The more bits in the word, the faster the computer can execute complicated tasks. The IBM PCs and compatibles are eight-bit while IBM ATs and 386-class computers are sixteen-bit. The Macintosh SE and Macintosh II family are thirty-two bit machines.

*RAM:* Random-access memory. This is the number of words that a computer can store for instantaneous retrieval without having to

go look for data on a disk drive. Generally, the more RAM a machine has, the faster it performs complex tasks and the more powerful the software it can handle. The bare minimum RAM required for a graphics computer is 1 mb (one megabyte or slightly more than 1 million bytes).

*ROM:* Read-only memory. These are silicon chips that store a computer's instruction set —the basic routines that individual software programs use to build complex features. ROMs are also sometimes used to hold software programs for portable computers. The computer can read the data in a ROM but can't write over or erase it. A computer's ROM usually contains highly-proprietary data. Manufacturers are very protective of their ROMs.

*Pixel:* Picture element. This is the basic unit of a graphics display (whether on a screen or on paper). Monitors (screens) are measured not only by the size of the screen, but by the number of pixels they display. This relates to the size of the document that can be seen at one time and to the apparent sharpness (resolution) of the image. The number of pixels per linear inch is equal to the resolution of the display in dots per inch (DPI). A bigger screen does not necessarily display a bigger document; it may spread a small document over a larger area, reducing its sharpness.

its pad; the pointer on the screen moves in the direction the mouse is rolling. Graphics computers allow you to draw, edit text, perform layout operations, even save files and enter instructions using a mouse instead of the keyboard. This is the proverbial "point and click" feature that early Macintosh ads referred to.

When you buy a graphics computer, take the mouse that comes with the machine. Until you develop your coordination a bit, you won't be able to tell the difference between a standard mouse and a more expensive one. Before upgrading, go to the computer dealer and try a trackball. A trackball is an upside-down mouse. You roll the ball with your fingers instead of rolling the mouse. If you have limited desk space, this can be a real wrist-saver. Some people say it's easier to draw with a mouse than a trackball; others say the trackball is easier.

### Tablets

There are a wide variety of drawing tablets available for graphics computers. These tablets are about one foot square (some are larger) and are wired so that their surface can sense the presence of an electronic pen. The pen can then be used much as you would use a pencil—to draw or to point to areas on the computer screen you wish to activate or modify. Some tablets come with a mouse-like device called a puck. The puck performs the same functions as a pen. Some models of tablets, pens, and pucks incorporate extra function buttons. If you will be doing a lot of illustration using the computer, consider buying a tablet and pen combination. The time saved by having the commands you use often (get pen, change line weight, save file) available at your fingertips might be worth the $150–$300 these devices cost. You don't absolutely need a tablet to do illustrations. It's really a matter of personal preference; some designers

like them and some don't. Try drawing with a mouse first, then find a dealer or another studio that has a tablet you can test drive.

### Other Input Devices

Once computer developers realized that there was a better way to talk to a computer than the old-fashioned keyboard, they began experimenting. Some of the ideas are quite promising, though none have really caught on with designers yet. Touch-sensitive screens are one option. By touching the screen with your finger, you can draw, move the cursor through text, and perform all of the functions usually done with a mouse.

There is also a touch-sensitive mini-tablet about the size of a postcard available for the Macintosh. It allows you to use your finger to move the pointer around the screen and to draw freehand using an electronic stylus. There are also voice input systems being developed. Already available, these use a microphone to pick up voice commands and relay them to the computer. You can "train" the computer to recognize dozens of common commands such as "open file," "close file," "go to page four," or "increase point size." At the time of publication, touch screens cost upwards of $600 and voice command systems cost upwards of $1,000. A little further out are pointing devices that use sensors mounted inside the fingers of a special glove. Look for prices on all of these units to plummet. Voice command systems would be extremely useful to designers, who often perform many repetitions of a fairly limited number of commands.

### Scanners

Scanners let you capture drawings, photographs, and other images from almost any source for manipulation in the computer. If you want to create position photos for your page layouts—to use in place of photostats—you'll need a scanner. Scanners are used extensively to provide base images that are then "traced over" and turned into illustrations in drawing programs.

Scanners "scan" a document or image, recording it as a series of "on" and "off" statements a computer can understand. You can use a scanner to capture line art, continuous tone art (paintings, photographs), or even text. Line art or continuous tone art can then be altered using an imaging program. The images can be placed into a page layout and printed as part of a mechanical, or the image can be printed directly to a laser printer or a high-resolution imagesetter. Text can be interpreted and saved as copy using OCR (Optical Copy Recognition) software.

*Image Scanners:* Scanners come in a variety of shapes and sizes. Unless you plan to work with nothing but line art or can live with positioning images that are very rough, buy a gray scale scanner. These are sometimes called "multi-bit" or "eight-bit" scanners. You want a scanner that will deliver 256 shades of gray. Some multi-bit scanners deliver only sixteen or sixty-four shades of gray.

Video digitizers are scanners that use a video camera (or video recorder) to capture the image to be scanned. Most video digitizers deliver 256 shades of gray.

*Scanning From Transparencies:* Conventional flatbed scanners work much like a photocopier. They only make copies from reflective photographs or artwork. A video scanner is very useful if you need images of three-dimensional objects or you make position images from transparencies. You can place a transparency on a light table, then focus the video camera on it.

*Scanning Text:* OCR sounds like the answer to every designer's dream. With a scanner and OCR software you should be able to take a client's manuscript, scan it, and save the results as a text file, ready to be poured into a brochure, ad, or book. Until 1989, OCR was spotty, at best. The software had trouble accurately reading text, especially typeset or multi-column text. Upgrades to existing programs and new packages released since 1989 have brought OCR up to a useful level, especially if your need is to scan a typewritten manuscript. You can, in fact, feed hard copy from your client into a scanner and receive an electronic text file, ready to be placed in a page layout.

*Scanning Color:* At this writing, several excellent low-cost color scanners were available for desktop graphics computers. Scanners capable of capturing 16.7 million colors at a resolution of 300–400 DPI were available for $2,000 to $6,000; scanners capable of capturing 16.7 million colors at 900 DPI were available for $9,000 to $15,000. Color-separation quality scanners were available for $20,000 and up. Video digitizers that provide full-color scans from video cameras were available for $900 to $3,000, but the resolution of the video camera limits their image quality.

## Monitors

Once you have a design in the computer, you have to be able to see it and print it—whether to paper, film, or videotape. That's what output devices are for. The most common output device is the CRT (cathode ray tube) monitor. A CRT is more or less a television screen that gets its signal from your computer instead of a television station. They come in a bewildering variety of sizes, configurations, and capabilities. (See page 156, *Rasters And Resolution.*)

Although there is a cost attached ($900–$2,000), we strongly advise buying a monitor large enough to display two letter-size pages side-by-side. A sixteen-inch monitor will suffice, but a nineteen-inch is preferable. The average CRT measures fourteen inches diagonally; the standard Macintosh Plus or Macintosh SE screen measures nine inches diagonally. Unless the majority of your work will be illustrations that fit on a small screen at 200 percent enlargement, you'll spend a lot of time scrolling around the screen to see different parts of your artwork if you have a small monitor. We've seen designers increase their productivity by a third when they moved up to a large monitor.

Aside from sizes, you'll also need to choose how many shades of gray or how many colors you want to see on screen. Monochrome monitors display only black and white (high contrast) images. They're suitable for most layout and publication work and are the least expensive. Grayscale monitors display up to 256 shades of gray, rendering colors and halftone photos in an appropriate shade of gray.

When manufacturers advertise color monitors, they don't necessarily mean photographic color. Low-priced color monitors ($550–$1,500) generally display no more than 256 colors at one time. True full-color monitors display 700,000 colors from a palette of 16.7 million colors and cost upwards of $2,000. They're useful if you produce full-color comps, color illustrations, color presentations, or video work.

Always ask the dealer if the monitor display board is included in the price he quotes you for a monitor. Except for the Macintosh SE and Plus (which have built-in monitors), your computer will need a monitor display board to generate the right video signal for the monitor you buy. Monitors are usually sold with a display board, but are sometimes priced separately.

## Printers

At some point, you're going to want to get ink on paper, so you'll need a printer. Again, there is a bewildering variety of makes and models.

For design and graphics, you can't get by with anything less than a PostScript-compatible laser printer (see page 152, *What Is PostScript?*). If you want access to a variety of quality, scalable fonts and to the advanced capabilities of the best drawing and painting programs, you need a PostScript laser. Dot-matrix and ink-jet printers just won't cut it. In 1989 two industry giants, Apple Computer and Microsoft, declared war on PostScript by announcing plans to develop their own page description standards. The advice above should be considered in light of any more recent developments in printing technology.

*Imagesetters:* A graphics computer can be connected directly to imagesetters made by Agfa/CompuGraphic, Linotronic, Birmy, and others. These are the same photocomposer units sold as dedicated typesetting systems. They can reproduce your files at very high resolutions (1270 DPI to 2450 DPI) on resin coated typesetting paper or on lithographic film.

*Color printers:* The currently available color printers are marvelous. The print quality is good enough for comps, but not good enough to judge color relationships. Their prices range from $5,000 to $30,000.

At 1990 prices, going to a minimal full-color system—color monitor, color scanner, color software, color printer—increased the price of a single-workstation graphics system from about $9,000 to $18,000 or more.

The advantage is that you can see your work in color and—more important—your clients can see your work in color.

The basic technology for the next generation of color printers is already in place. Look for devices that will be able to deliver Chromalin-quality images directly from a desktop graphics computer. These printers use a dye sublimation process that is capable of very fine results, rather than the thermal wax ink used by older color printers. DuPont has released a dye sublimation printer for use as a pre-press proofing device, but it was priced at $75,000 at the time of this writing. Prices on this technology should gradually decrease: Kodak released a dye sublimation printer for $25,000 in the spring of 1990, and Mitsubishi offered a desktop unit for $6,000.

### Film Recorders

Film recorders put computer images onto conventional photographic film. Most will accept both transparency films for 35mm slides and color negative films. If you produce presentations, a film recorder can be a quick way to recoup some of your investment.

At publication time film recorders that make acceptable-quality 35mm slides (4,000 lines of resolution) were available for less than $5,000.

Film recorders could become an excellent medium for graphics studios. Recorders capable of creating 4x5 inch transparencies with the same resolution as a 35mm Kodachrome slide are available. In 1990, the prices were astronomical: The MDA-1000, for example, went for $200,000. Don't despair. In 1980, equipment capable of animating color images on a computer screen cost $200,000. By 1988, the price had fallen to less than $20,000.

### Storage Options

After you create all those wonderful files, you have to store them somewhere. The bad news is that the average size of graphics software files is growing explosively. In 1987, a software program that was 600 kb in size was considered huge. Today, 600 kb is average and programs that run to 1.5 mb aren't unknown. The data files these programs create are large, too. For example, grayscale scans of photographs average 300 kb. Ten photographs equal 3 mb. Thirty photographs would completely fill a 10 mb hard disk. Color

files are even larger; a scan of a single color photograph can easily fill 4 mb. Color separators commonly deal with files of 40 mb for a single color image. Get as much disk storage as you can afford. At the time of publication, a 40 mb hard disk was the bare minimum for a graphics computer. Sixty megabytes is preferable, and 100 mb should give you some elbow room to keep a variety of illustrations on file.

The good news is that prices on hard disk drives dropped precipitously between 1987 and 1990. In 1987, a 20 mb hard disk drive for a Macintosh computer cost $1,200. In early 1990, that same $1,200 would buy a 100 mb hard disk.

"Hard" disks are more properly called Winchester hard disk drives. Reputedly, they were named Winchesters by a researcher at IBM because the first models would store 30 mb on each side (30/30). The Winchester .30-.30 is a popular sporting rifle.

Disk drives that use interchangeable 20 mb or 45 mb disk cartridges are worth a look. They allow you to move big files around easily, say, between your studio and an output bureau. Many service bureaus use the 45 mb models as their "standard" for data exchange.

New storage options are constantly being developed. Some of the more promising are:

*WORM:* Write-once-read-many. This device uses a laser and an optical disk, like an audio compact disk player, to write data. However, once written, it can't be erased or written over. When the disk is full, you need to plug in a new disk. WORM drives come in sizes up to 650 mb and are priced from $3,500 and up.

*REO:* Like a WORM drive, an REO uses an optical disk and a laser. Unlike a WORM, it's possible to erase or write over the data, just like on a conventional hard disk. These, too, come in sizes up to 650 mb as well as "jukebox" models that hold several 650 mb cartridges Prices are comparable to those for WORM drives.

# The Heart Of It All: The Software

What a graphics computer can do for you depends on whether the software available for your particular machine can perform the tasks you desire. The instructions used by a computer—the list of operations to be performed—is called software, as opposed to hardware, which is the machinery itself. See page 76, *Read 'Em And Weep* for specific advice on how to make sure the gear you buy will actually do the job you want.

Computer capabilities change very fast. New software programs are released rapidly and existing programs are upgraded constantly, adding to their functionality. At this point, don't be concerned about which specific programs you should buy. Instead, concentrate on matching the kinds of tasks you want a computer to do with the available software and hardware.

Graphics software comes in a number of basic flavors—PageMaker® and Quark XPress® are both page layout programs, for example—and the major programs within each category tend to be somewhat equal in the features they offer.

## Page Layout Programs

*What they do:* Page layout programs—PageMaker, Quark XPress, Ventura Publisher®, Ready Set Go®, and the like—are the electronic equivalent of both a phototypesetter and a drawing board. If you deliver your work as mechanical boards with type in place, page layout programs will be your mainstay. They allow you to design pages with all type and images in place and output them as single-page mechanicals.

*How they work:* These programs put a replica of a mechanical board (the "page") on the computer screen. Then, using a variety of electronic tools, you establish the image area, draw rules, set type, size and position line art or halftones created in other software programs, place screens, and resize and rearrange the elements at will. Most allow you to work with multi-page documents (such as two-sided cards, brochures, and books) and even make global changes (such as changing all subheads from italic to bold) throughout a document with one command. When you're satisfied with what you have, the pages can be printed on a laser printer for a low-resolution proof or printed on a high-resolution phototypesetter for use as camera-ready art.

*What about fonts?* In the beginning (that is, way back in 1984) there were only a handful of fonts available and they couldn't be output to an imagesetter for use as reproduction type. By January 1990, there were more than 1,000 fonts available from leading digital type foundries including Adobe and Bitstream. The fonts are the same ones you're used to getting from your conventional typesetter, many produced under license from International Typeface Corporation and other well-known foundries, with true-cut italics, condensed, and expanded faces. There are, of course, many more than 1,000 typefaces available for conventional phototypesetters, but these are rapidly becoming available for use on desktop computers. The major foundries have committed themselves to offering the bulk of their libraries for use on graphics computers. Letraset also offers many of its LetraGraphica® dry transfer typefaces in digital form and is releasing new fonts rapidly.

The most surprising (and distressing) thing about font packages is their cost. Adobe, one of the first suppliers of digital fonts for desktop machines, prices font packages from $85 to $375. Each package generally includes a roman, italic, bold, and bold italic of one typeface; the more expensive packages include extended font families, such as four weights of Helvetica. Apple LaserWriter laser printers are shipped with 35 basic typefaces (Apple counts Bookman and Bookman Bold as two faces). Unless you plan to do nothing but illustrations, buy at least five additional font packages to start your library, then reserve some funds to buy new fonts regularly. The costs are not inconsiderable, but compared to the cost of rerunning galleys (not to mention the time required to send type back to a typesetter and wait for it to be rerun), it's an investment you can recoup if you don't buy fonts you don't really need.

Much has been said about the suitability of type generated using a graphics computer. Typesetting involves more than merely typing in the words. Graphics computers offer typographic controls of the same type, variety, and power as those used on dedicated phototypesetters. If you want to spend the time kerning letter pairs down to 1/200th of an em, as a typesetter might,

you can get the same results. If you have a vast body of copy that has to be set just so, you'll either have to learn how typesetters use the available controls to make that happen, or you'll have to hire a typesetter. Only poor craftsmen blame their tools. Good results—as good as the type you'll find in any well-designed national magazine—can be achieved using a desktop system. In fact, a number of magazines produce their type on desktop systems.

*Importing text:* The more sophisticated programs allow you to import text created in a word processing program and place it within a page. This will be useful if you set long blocks of text for your clients. Instead of marking up their manuscript and sending it to a typesetter, if your

---

### QUALITY COUNTS: Phototypesetters Versus Graphics Computers

As designers, we've been trained to think that nothing less than a dedicated phototypesetter can generate quality type.

That was true in 1986, but it's not true today. Graphics computers being sold now have more type-manipulation capabilities and more raw processing power than the dedicated phototypesetters being sold in 1980. The reason? All phototypesetters are driven by computers. And the basic building blocks of computers—silicon chips—have decreased in price by a factor of ten while their power has increased by a factor of ten. In 1980, a phototypesetter with 128 kilobytes of random access memory (RAM) was considered a very powerful machine. The least expensive Apple Macintosh available today comes standard with 1 megabyte (1,000 kilobytes) of RAM.

Many of the arguments advanced by traditionalists against desktop-generated type are the same arguments heard in the late 1960s

when typesetters converted from hot-metal machines to phototype. We all survived that transition; we'll survive this one, too. You really won't have a choice. Just as there are today only a very few type shops that set type in hot metal, within this decade type shops that do not use microcomputers as input devices will be the exception. The reason is simple: Microcomputers cost less than dedicated typesetting input stations.

It's true that there's a price to be paid to unlock all of that power: You'll have to learn how to manipulate type. You'll need to become familiar with kerning pairs, justification methods, and the dozen or so controls that determine how tightly lines are spaced, where hyphenations occur, and so on. If you spend a few hours with your page layout program—or hire someone who will—you can learn to produce type that replicates what you've been getting from your typesetter.

client can supply you with the text on a computer disk in any one of a number of common formats (ASCII, WordStar®, WordPerfect®, MicroSoft Word®, or MacWrite®), you can pick up the text from disk, put it on a page, and change the face, size, leading, and column width without having to retype it.

Also, here's where the more expensive programs can actually save you money: If you buy a good page layout program, you may not need a word processing program. Especially if your need is for typesetting and page make-up—as opposed to writing long documents—the word processing features of some page layout programs may be entirely adequate. Although we have two of the leading word processing packages, we don't use them. All of our writing—letters, memos, proposals, even book-length manuscripts—is done in our page layout program. It has almost all the features of a dedicated word processing program—global search-and-replace, style sheets, and a spelling checker—plus some features most word processors lack, such as multiple-level zoom display, font

search-and-replace, and multiple kerning tables. It does not have automatic page numbering nor does it automatically footnote a long document as the most expensive word processors do.

If you'll be using a telecommunications package to send mail to your clients electronically, you will need a rudimentary word processor to create the mail. Most "desk utility" packages, such as Borland SideKick®, include a functional word processor suitable for writing short notes and letters up to five pages.

***Advanced features:*** Some programs support features such as multiple kerning tables with hundreds of kerning pairs per table; the ability to wrap type around complex shapes; to import graphics directly into a page from a scanner without having to go through a scanning program first; automatic alignment of text throughout a multi-page document; screening of text in percentages of gray or matching text to Pantone® colors; and the ability to directly print separation negatives for spot color screens and type.

A few very sophisticated programs allow you to place and size four-color photographs into

## But I Don't Want To Set Type

Surprise. Typesetters do more than just type words onto a screen. You *can* save time and money by setting your own type, but you should take the time to learn some of the tricks of the trade:

☐ At the very least, learn to kern and track headlines. The training time is well worth the improvement you'll get in quality.

☐ Ask clients to submit long blocks of copy on disk rather than as manuscript.

☐ Find someone with typesetting experience to type copy on an as-needed basis.

☐ Ask your phototype service bureau if they will type copy from your clients' manuscript and provide it to you on disk for use in your layouts.

☐ Read a book on the basics of producing professional-quality type from a microcomputer. Several titles are listed on page 158 of the *Resources* section.

your layouts and combine them with color tints, line art, and text. These can be output as composed film—ready to plate and run on a four-color press—through a high-end separation system such as a Crosfield, Hell, or Scitex. More programs should gain this ability as the software developers add support for the Open Pre-Press Interface (OPI). OPI is a set of file format specifications that allow these high-end color systems to read the page dimensions, type specifications, screen densities, and so on directly from your page layout file. See page 154, *Color From The Desktop*, for more details.

There are some things all layout programs ought to do but which most of them won't. At the time of publication, only one major layout package, Xpress® 3.0, let users rotate text and illustrations at any angle of their choice. The most recent upgrade of PageMaker does allow text to be rotated 90 degrees.

There are "workaround" solutions for this (cutting angled type in by hand or using a drawing program to convert the type to a piece of line art, then rotating it, and placing it on the page as a graphic). Most programs do not let you rotate graphics, either; if you want a photo angled, you have to rotate it in a photo retouching program first, then import it into a layout.

Currently, none of the packages let you set text along an arbitrary baseline, such as around a curve. Several auxiliary programs will let you set type at angles, around curves, inside circles, or along any arbitrary baseline; but you have to convert the text to a graphic and place it into the page as a piece of line art. If you want to make a correction or change in that text, you can't edit it easily—it has to be recreated in the auxiliary program.

An integrated grammar checker, which could check the type in page layouts for obvious mistakes such as repeated words and faulty punctuation would be a boon, too.

## Drawing/Painting Software

*What they do:* Drawing and painting software takes the place of pencil, paper, and paint. The drawing and painting software available for graphics computers is really first class. The standouts in the Macintosh world, Adobe Illustrator® and Aldus FreeHand®, have set a very high standard for illustration software. If your work is primarily rendering spot illustrations and creating logos, you'll spend most of your computer time working with one of these packages.

*How they work:* Drawing programs replicate a pad and pencil. They present you with an electronic page on which you use a mouse or electronic pen to draw straight lines, curved lines, and a variety of shapes (*e.g.* circles, squares, polygons). These shapes can be shaded in values of gray or—if you have a color monitor—in Pantone or process colors. You can combine type with your illustrations and even manipulate that type in a variety of ways; condensing, outlining, binding the baseline to a curve, shading, or turning it into a three-dimensional object.

Some programs also allow you to scan photographs or objects, then automatically trace the outline of the object. If you were creating a drawing that included a vase, for example, you could scan in a photo of a vase, use the trace feature, then clean up the tracing using the drawing tools. This scan-and-trace feature doesn't work very well for objects you want to represent in three dimensions. It does, however, produce two-dimensional outlines well. If you have a client who has lost the original art for his logo, it would be reasonably simple to scan it in from a piece of letterhead, trace it, then clean up the outline. Some designers use this feature to trace over thumbnails of their most promising ideas. Generally, the auto-tracing features work best on objects with simple outlines. An aerial photo of the fiords of Norway could take hours for the software to trace and might result in an image with many stray lines. In this instance, it might be faster to put the photo on a light box and trace it by hand. The tracing could then be scanned into the computer for further manipulation.

Some illustration programs will produce gradient "fills," also called "fountains" or "ramps." This is a tint screen (whether gray or some other color), that increases in density in one direction. An example is a radial fill, in which the color in the center is fully saturated, but fades by degrees to pure white at the edges of the circle. These fills can be put into the outline of type, inside of shapes, across a whole page; just about anywhere. The software gives a great deal of control over the fills, letting you specify the starting and ending values (0 to 100 percent or 50 to 70 percent, for example) and the number of steps in which you'd like the change to take place. The greater the number of steps, the smoother the transition between values. Specifying a radial fill with four steps inside of a six-inch circle will give you something that looks like a dart board. Specifying 256 steps over the same distance will render a very smooth fade from black in the center to white at the edges.

These fills can produce effects similar to that created by an airbrush. While none of the illustrators we spoke with had completely abandoned their airbrushes, they rated the computer as very good. In some instances, such as when producing a gradient fade from blue to yellow, some illustrators felt the computer produced a cleaner result than a traditional airbrush. For other tasks, especially where a gradient tint needs to be applied to a three-dimensional curve, some felt the airbrush was a better solution.

Since it isn't possible to make reproduction-quality transparencies of art created in these drawing programs, several illustrators said they send their illustrations to clients as process color separations or as an electronic file. The file can be sent via modem to a client's computer, elimi-

nating the delay (and expense) of an air-express package. The downside, they said, is that they prefer to work with their own service bureau to make sure the separations are output properly.

Drawing programs are frequently used to create logotypes. By scanning in type and tracing over it, or by directly opening PostScript font outlines from an auxiliary program, designers can quickly manipulate type in ways that take great skill and a lot of time when done with conventional methods.

One very important distinction to make when comparing illustration programs is whether they produce bit-mapped or vector graphics. The difference is important.

***Bit-mapped graphics*** are images which are simply a pixel-by-pixel reiteration of what appeared on your computer screen. The computer "remembers" the illustration as a checkerboard of pixels that are "on" or "off." The disadvantage to this scheme is that the dimensions of the illustrations are fixed, limited by the total number of pixels displayed on your monitor. If you bring the illustration into a page layout and enlarge it 200 percent, the image quality will plummet. The checkerboard of pixels (now twice as large as before) will be very obvious, and your curves will have a jagged, stair-step appearance. Printing on a high-resolution imagesetter won't improve the quality of the image.

***Vector images*** are stored by the computer as a series of lines, curves, angles, and planes. Illustrator, FreeHand, and other programs produce vector graphics. They are often referred to by the software developers as PostScript graphics, because PostScript is the computer language the vectors are encoded in. When imported into a page layout, they can be scaled to any dimension without affecting their image quality. When printed on an imagesetter, their quality improves, printing at the highest resolution available on that printer.

## Font Manipulation

*What they do:* In 1990, several developers released packages that allowed designers to use the outlines of PostScript fonts (such as those from Adobe and Bitstream) as line art. This may seem obvious, but until these packages were released, designers had to "draw over" letters or words with the mouse—much as you would with a piece of tracing paper—to get a line art file that could then be further altered using a drawing program.

The advantage of this new software is that it makes altering letters from an existing alphabet much easier. Using the wide array of tools in a drawing program, designers can create custom alphabets and logotypes much more quickly than they can using a photostat and a technical pen. Other packages that facilitate the creation of custom lettering and logotypes have appeared as well, such as TypeStyler®, TypeAlign®, and LetraStudio®. These packages support various features such as binding type to an arbitrary outline, skewing type, and creating three-dimensional letters or symbols.

Fontographer®, a program that has been around for several years, allows designers to create their own PostScript typefaces from scratch, or by starting with an existing face and modifying it. The typefaces can be used in page layouts and printed on a high-resolution imagesetter. Several magazines reported they used Fontographer® to create special condensed versions of their text face. Like the other font manipulation packages, it can also be used to create logos.

Logos created with these programs are PostScript art. You can keep them in an electronic file and place them in any document—a frame destined for output as a 35mm slide for a presentation, in a print brochure, or even on a frame of videotape. This eliminates the need to keep multiple photostats of client logos on file.

## Scanning

*What they do:* Scanning programs add the capabilities of a stat camera to your computer. Used with a scanner, they can capture line art or photographs and put them into a computer file. You can then alter or rotate the file, or use it as the basis for an entirely new illustration. The technology was slow in developing but took off in 1988 and 1989. In the first quarter of 1987, there were two photo imaging programs for the Macintosh; by the first quarter of 1990, there were more than twenty.

Scans can be made from flat art (line art, tracings, or photographs) or, with special attachments, from transparencies (see page 37, *Scanners*).

*How they work:* Scanning software takes data coming from a scanner—an input device that "reads" a photo and turns it into a pattern of dots—and puts it into a file format that can be used by your computer and by your other software packages. There are a number of file formats: TIFF, PICT, RIFF, and EPSF are among the most common. These programs are often sold in conjunction with a particular brand of scanner. Most have some rudimentary image manipulation controls—brightness, contrast, cut-and-paste, rotation—but no real ability to retouch or alter photographs significantly.

Using a scanning program, you'll capture an image from the scanner and save it as a separate electronic file. When buying this software, be sure that at least one of the formats supported by the scanning software is compatible with your page layout software. Don't take a salesman's word for this. Confirm it directly with the software manufacturer and try importing a scan yourself on a rental or demonstration machine.

These programs may support one-bit scanning or multi-bit scanning. If your scanner and scanning software support only one-bit, you will be able to capture and manipulate images much as

## QUALITY PHOTOGRAPHIC IMAGES: Still Developing

It is possible to import, retouch, and output quality photographic images—continuous-tone or halftone (separation)—using desktop computers. However, at this time, it can't be done using the low-priced (under $2,000) equipment.

The imaging software is pretty capable, although it's still behind what's available for commercial color separation stations. The biggest shortcomings are in input devices (scanners) and output devices (printers).

The lower-priced gear is good enough to provide positioning images for your printer in place of traditional photostats. It isn't yet good enough to make halftone or separation film of photographs for your printer, unless a job requires nothing more than small, not-too-detailed halftones or small color photographs.

The reasons for this are covered in more detail on page 154, *Color From The Desktop*.

High-quality separations and halftones can be made from files created on desktop computers, but at this time, it requires a dedicated system or moving the desktop files into a traditional high-end pre-press system for scanning and output. Magazine-quality separations can be made now. (See page 154 and the illustration on page sixteen.)

Some service bureaus convert desktop files to plate-ready composite film with photographic separations in place. We've been quoted prices ranging from $175 per page to $500 per page for this service. Utilizing the service also requires at minimum a color video board for your computer ($900–$3,500) and a color monitor ($550–$5,000). To use this service effectively, you'd probably also want to buy a color scanner ($1,800-$12,000) and a color printer ($5000-$25,000) to make rough page proofs.

Currently, there's no good way of outputting reproduction-quality continuous-tone images directly from a desktop computer onto paper. The DuPont 4Cast and Kodak XL7700 due sublimation printers may change that. It is possible to output reasonably high-resolution images to a film recorder, which makes a color transparency or negative. The negative or slide can then be used just like a conventional photograph for projection, making color prints, or separation. Film recorders capable of capturing images with a resolution of 4,000 lines cost $5,000 to $12,000.

Making direct comparisons between traditional photographic materials and computer (digital) materials is very tricky. According to figures provided by Eastman Kodak, a 35mm Kodachrome 25 slide has a resolution of approximately 100 lines/millimeter. It would take a computer file containing 18 million pixels to match the visual sharpness of a Kodachrome slide. The sharpest 35mm film recorders—the 4,000 line models—produce images that contain about 12 million pixels. Some large-format film recorders can produce 4x5 inch transparencies from files with 20 million pixels.

You needn't buy a film recorder to output images to film, however. Service bureaus that make transparencies from your computer files are widely available. Prices range from $7 to $20, depending on location and service. Check the computer magazines for addresses.

If you work in videotape, excellent video output devices and animation packages are available at reasonable prices.

you would with a photostat camera using high-contrast paper: There will be no shades of gray in your images. The software may allow you to simulate the shades of gray in a photograph by a process called dithering. If your primary use for a scanner and imaging software will be to capture line art, with only an occasional photo to stat, a one-bit scanner may be a money-saving option. If you work with photographs often and want to use your scanner for positioning images on your mechanicals, a grayscale (multi-bit) scanner and software are the best choice. See page 156, *Rasters And Resolution*, for more information.

*Shades Of Gray:* Multi-bit scanners allow you to capture black, white, *and* gray. With a four-bit scanner, you can capture and display sixteen different gray values; an eight-bit scanner captures 256 different gray values. When printed on a high-resolution phototypesetter, an eight-bit scan can look much like a black and white photograph. True magazine-quality halftones are still beyond the reach of the most common desktop scanners and software (see *Quality Photographic Images*, opposite).

*Full Color:* Color scanners and scanning software usually come in eight-bit, twenty-four bit, and thirty-two bit configurations. An eight-bit color scanner allows you to capture 256 colors. A twenty-four or thirty-two bit scanner will record 16.7 million colors at 256 brightness values. The results, when viewed on a full-color monitor, look as good as—usually better than—a network television broadcast. See page 154, *Color From The Desktop.*

## Retouching Programs

Since 1988, developers have released a number of programs that allow you to retouch photographs much as you would with an airbrush or a high-end imaging system such as Scitex or Quantel. While capabilities vary, they generally offer the ability to cut-and-paste images, to pick up and duplicate image values from one part of an image to another, and to "draw" on top of the photo using electronic brushes, pencils, airbrushes, water droplets (for smudging hard edges or blending a seam where two different values meet), and so on. While most of these programs work only with black and white art, several excellent packages designed specifically for manipulating color images are available.

The most sophisticated of these color retouching programs—Adobe PhotoShop®, Letraset ColorStudio®, PhotoMac®, SpectrePrint®—already offer the ability to produce true photographic four-color separations directly from a graphics computer. By early 1990, the results were extremely impressive. Desktop machines were being used to make magazine-quality separations, and higher-quality separations were being made using a combination of desktop and high-end workstations. As of April 1990, the color photographs for *MacWeek*, an industry trade tabloid owned by Ziff-Davis Publishing Company, were being scanned and separated on desktop equipment. Quality four-color separations should become commonplace as the power of the software and the quality of affordable color scanners increase.

## Presentations

The era of "desktop presentations," creating multi-media information and entertainment on a graphics computer, is upon us. Traditionally, multi-media has been the domain of audio-visual specialists, photographers, and sound recordists.

Corporations, in particular, have long recognized the persuasive power of a good multi-media presentation. The use of overhead projectors, video, slides, and hand-outs can turn a complex, mundane business proposal into an eye-catching, easy-to-understand light-and-sound show. In most cases, pictures and words together communicate a lot better than do words alone.

Basic software for creating multi-media presentations on a graphics computer has been around since 1986, but truly industrial-strength packages didn't appear until 1988. One of their advantages over traditional methods of production is that all of the elements needed for a presentation—slides, video, sound, printed copies—can be prepared on one machine. The PostScript language gives you the ability to print the documents created in a presentation program to a 35mm film recorder, videotape, or an imagesetter for lithographic reproduction. There is no need to separately set the type and draw illustrations for the slides, handouts, and video. In fact, there may not be a need for slides at all, as a graphics computer can be hooked up to a projection television or to an oversized monitor. The presentation software can be programmed to "cycle" through the show just as a traditional sequencer for a slide projector would. Numerous accessories, from infra-red keyboard controllers to liquid-crystal panels that fit on top of an overhead projector in place of a traditional transparency, are available.

Some designers expect desktop presentations to become a major, and lucrative, market for design studios. However, don't dismiss the very real skills that traditional A/V specialists possess. Adding a graphics computer to your studio won't make you an A/V expert. You'll need the skills to visually communicate—not merely decorate—your client's message.

### Spreadsheets / Graphing Programs

**What they do:** Spreadsheet programs replace an accountant's ledger sheet and a calculator. Graphing programs build graphs automatically from numbers you type in.

Too few designers take advantage of the really excellent spreadsheet and graphing programs. They can be used for both design projects and as management tools to estimate job costs, track expenses, manage client databases, and even keep the books straight.

*How they work:* On the screen, a spreadsheet displays a large tic-tac-toe chart with a huge number of columns and rows. Specific features vary, but at a minimum, the programs perform a wide variety of sophisticated operations on numbers (or words) typed into the chart. Simple addition, subtraction, multiplication, and division are just the beginning; many programs can figure the lease payments for a piece of equipment without you having to know anything more than the cost of the equipment, the interest rate and how many months you want the lease to run. They can also do things like net present value and future value of assets.

*Graphing:* Many spreadsheets offer graphing. Lotus 1-2-3® (the mainstay of IBM-compatible computers) and Excel® (for the Macintosh) are real workhorse spreadsheets capable of tackling the most complex statistical project. Their graphing capabilities are good, but basic, offering several variations of pie charts, stacked-bar graphs, line, area, and scatter plots. WingZ® and Trapeze® (both for Macintosh) were designed specifically for the visual display of data and can quickly generate a huge variety of charts and graphs. The graphs can be saved in a file format that can then be imported into a page layout program and printed on a phototypesetter.

Tables and charts, an onerous chore even for an experienced typesetter, can be produced using a spreadsheet and then flowed into a page layout document. Most spreadsheets allow you to save their contents as text files. To create a table, you type in the headings across the top and the categories down the side. Then fill in your words or numbers in the little boxes in between. When you save the spreadsheet as a text file, the program will put tab returns in between the words that appeared in the boxes. The tabs can then be set wherever you want in your page layout program. It's not quite an instant chart, but it's close. Some spreadsheets also allow you to save word or number charts as graphics that can then be placed in a page layout just like an illustration or photograph.

There are many advanced wrinkles in these programs: Using the Microsoft Works® series of software products (which includes a spreadsheet and a quasi-page layout program), it's possible to "hot-link" spreadsheets to a layout—that is, changes made to a spreadsheet are automatically updated in the text. This could be useful if you do a lot of work in the financial or annual reports fields. Charts and graphs can be updated automatically as the layout is being worked on.

There are also products designed specifically to create graphs. Cricket Graph® is one of the established products that runs on both IBM-compatible and Macintosh computers. The graphs for this book were created in Cricket Graph, saved as graphics, and then pasted into a page layout.

Creating a basic graph in either a spreadsheet or graphing program is very easy; you simply type in the numbers to be plotted (e.g. years versus income figures) and then choose what type of graph you want from a menu. Most graphing programs also import data from the leading spreadsheet programs. Numbers from a spreadsheet containing projected annual revenues and expenses, for example, can be transferred into the graphing program and graphed. Generally, you have a choice of patterns to fill bars, pie sections, or lines with. The graph is drawn on your screen pretty quickly and can be printed to a laser printer for closer scrutiny. Fine tuning the graph takes a little more time. The method of changing typefaces and positioning type is

inconvenient and imprecise in some packages. Also, because the type is saved as a graphic, rather than as text, you can't edit the text once you've placed the chart in your page layout unless the programs are "hot linked."

***Your Money Matters, Too:*** Spreadsheets are among the most useful business accessories a studio owner or freelancer can buy. Aside from automating routine financial calculations—such as job estimates—they can open the way for the non-accounting inclined to get a handle on budgeting, financing, and profitability. Ironically, few designers tap this power. You may ultimately decide to hire an outside accountant to keep an eye on your fiscal well-being, but if you want quick access to your financial data, or are on a limited budget, a spreadsheet can be an excellent business tool.

At the very least, if you quote jobs that are in any way complicated, buy a spreadsheet package and set up a spreadsheet to do your pricing. If you know how much type costs per page of output, how much you want to charge per hour of design time, and how much your general office expenses are, you'll find yourself forecasting profits much more accurately. Once you own a spreadsheet program, you can buy pre-fabricated spreadsheets that estimate job costs, taxes, expenses, and so on. We even found a group of templates created by a freelance designer. When you have an estimate sheet set up in the computer, as each new job comes in, you simply key in the appropriate numbers—of pages, design hours—and it calculates your real costs, what your price should be, and the resulting net profit after deducting general business expenses.

The spreadsheet estimate is also a good budget minder: Print out the spreadsheet for each job and keep it handy, checking your progress on the job against the estimates you used to price it. This will give you an early warning when you start going over budget with time or materials.

### Billing And Accounting

***What they do:*** Billing programs keep track of the hours you spend on each job. Accounting programs replace the traditional ledger-and-checkbook method of accounting.

Despite the huge investment in Macintosh computers among the various studios we spoke with, very few used their graphics computers to perform business functions. Some already had business data on IBM-compatible computers before buying a Macintosh for graphics and saw no reason to change. Others do their business chores manually or have an outside accountant.

There are now several software programs, including TimeSlips® and DesignSoft®, that allow you to track the amount of time spent on each job by each designer. These are a terrific way of tracking the billable hours generated by each designer and of analyzing which of your accounts are the most profitable and which are losers. One designer uses DesignSoft to track the time budgeted for a project against how much time her designers are spending on it.

"It allowed me to see which accounts weren't profitable for our studio and why," said Pat Davis. The Sacramento-based designer said she has taken the numbers generated by the computer to her clients, using them as the basis for renegotiating fees.

"I've never had a client turn down my request for renegotiating fees when I've had this data in hand," she said. 'They can see for themselves, in black and white, why their projects cost more to produce."

More information on accounting software for design studios can be found on pages 141–145.

### Telecommunications

***What they do:*** Communications programs work with a modem to encode your computer files so they can be transmitted over a telephone line. Sending files—text, layouts, even mechanicals to be typeset—over the phone is a quick and inexpensive way to move designs long distances. The cost of a modem is minimal and communications software is easy to operate. It's possible to have clients send you text over a phone line, put it into a page layout, and zap it back to them literally within minutes and without leaving your desk. You can also send files to be typeset to a service bureau around the corner or around the world by telephone without leaving your desk. If you work with a local service bureau, you can send line corrections or rush files over the phone, then have the type delivered. If you work with a bureau long distance, you can send the file to them by telephone and have type or film delivered by express courier the next morning.

Facsimile circuit boards, which allow your computer to send files directly to a facsimile machine without your having to print them out first, can be a time-saver. If you now send rough illustrations, layouts, copy, or copies of mechanicals by facsimile, seriously consider a fax board or a fax modem.

Telecommunications is one way to work around incompatible computer systems. If your clients have IBM-compatible gear and you have a Macintosh, the modem is a way to get their text into your machine. This is because there is a standard language for computer communications; a file format known as ASCII. Getting clients to use their modems is more difficult than actually transmitting or receiving the files. If your clients subscribe to MCI Mail, an electronic mail system, you can send full layouts, complete with type and images, to MCI where your client can pick them up at their leisure.

Communications packages are relatively inexpensive; many modems come with software. Full-featured communications packages cost less than $200 and good packages are available for less than $100.

# Chapter Three:
# A New Way Of Working

**A New Way Of Thinking And Working**

**Changing The Way You Work**

**Taking Responsibility
For The Technical Details**

## A New Way Of Thinking And Working

By itself, purchasing a graphics computer ensures nothing—except that your bank balance will decline. As good as these machines are, they're a long, long way from having the intelligence and reasoning ability of the average six-year-old. To date, no one has developed a robotic art assistant with six arms and a repertoire of stylistic sensibilities ranging from Rembrandt to Rauschenberg.

In order to reap the benefits about which the manufacturers and computer magazines rhapsodize at such great length, *you* have to *adapt*: adapt the computer hardware and software to your specific needs, and most importantly, adapt the way you approach projects to the computer's skills and abilities.

Certainly you can purchase a graphics computer and use it for things that neatly fit into your existing work flow and work style. Many studios have found this a workable compromise between being completely traditional and completely digital shops. But to reap the biggest savings and make the largest gains in productivity,

you have to make a commitment to transferring as many functions as possible to the computer. (See page 115 for a flow chart analysis).

Analysis, however, must wait. First, you have to decide if this is a commitment that you *want* to make. Consultants who specialize in graphics workstations can tell you what's *possible* to do; only you know what you're *willing* to do.

The biggest changes are in the nature of the computer as a tool, in the timing and flow of work in your studio, and in the responsibilities—for training yourself and gaining technical knowledge—you'll need to take on.

### Hand Jive

Look around your studio and you'll find an infinite variety of hand tools. There's something familiar, comforting, and even inspiring in the way a pastel stick lays color on a piece of D'Arches paper or in the precision of a fine ruling pen. There's a sense of control. There's a certain amount of tactile feedback; the vibrations

---

### Different Strokes

Lance Hidy is a well-known New England artist, designer, and illustrator. In addition to a healthy graphic design practice, he operates Mink Brook Editions, a fine art silk screen printing and publishing company, with his partner, Rob Day.

Actually Hidy has two partners; the other is an Apple Macintosh II® computer. Until he was 43, Hidy did his illustrations with traditional tools: pencil, brush, photocopy, photostat. But that was B.C. (before the computer). Since 1988, virtually all of his illustrations have been produced on the Mac.

"Using a mouse to form an image with Bezier

(bee-zee-*ay'*) curves in Adobe Illustrator® is not the same as drawing with a pencil," Hidy affirms. "I like the way a pencil feels on paper.

"Drawing with the computer can be tedious. However, once I have the image input, I can manipulate it in ways that are impossible when drawing by hand. I can change the line weights instantly, and if I don't like the effect, change them back. Or I can quickly rework part of the drawing. I can stroke and fill areas with just a few keyboard commands. I used to get my satisfaction from doing the actual drawing. Now I get the same kind of satisfaction by working with the image after it's drawn."

coming through the pen tickle the nerves in your fingers a certain way when the pen is making a smooth, straight line. It just *feels* right.

Like other fine craftsmen, artists are attached to the way their tools handle, to the way they feel.

When you begin working on a graphics computer, you'll have to give up some of that satisfaction. Drawing with a pen is visceral—it involves the sense of touch, of sight, of sound. Drawing with a computer is much more cerebral. There's certainly a great deal of "touch" involved in drawing a smooth curve with a mouse, but it feels completely different. The emphasis is less on the act of drawing and more on the conception of the line—where it should be placed and how it fits into the overall structure of the electronic file. The steps are identical: you look, you judge, you draw, you evaluate. Now the judging and evaluating outweigh the drawing itself. The good news is that revisions are much, much easier with a computer. You can play with the line after you've drawn it, changing weight, angle, curve, color, and stroke quickly and at will.

There are similar differences for other tasks you should consider moving onto the computer. Paste-up no longer involves a table, T-square, and knife. Working over a mechanical board until it's just right is undeniably arduous, but it can also be satisfying. Also, the feedback is immediate and obvious. A picture that's slightly crooked will hit your eye immediately when you're looking at the mechanical lying on a table. The tilt might not be as readily apparent when the mechanical is viewed on a computer monitor, which has a curved screen.

Similarly, the cure is fast and easy on a drafting board: Just grab the photostat and align it with the T-square. In an electronic file, you might have to close your layout program, open a graphics program, rotate the photo by typing in the number of degrees it is out of alignment,

then save it, reopen the layout, and paste it in. The process is simpler than it sounds, and the time saved in lining up columns of type (and especially in the ability to resize the photos at will without going back to the photocopier or photostat machine) more than makes up for such minor inconveniences. The current version of Quark XPress® (v3.0) allows users to rotate text and graphics without having to exit to another program, and the developers of the other major packages shouldn't be too far behind.

Mechanics aside, the time you now spend with a T-square and ruling pen is going to be spent sitting in front of a computer monitor. You're the one who has to decide if you want to make that change.

The graph on the following page gives an idea about how much of your workday will be affected. For example, the third step, specifying type, is something you now do with a stack of manuscript and a pen. You look at type books, pick your typefaces, then imagine the relationship between weights and sizes and write instructions to the typesetter on the manuscript.

With a graphics computer, you'll still have to find the right typeface, but you can do it by actually experimenting with type right on your screen, in position, in your rough layout. If one combination doesn't work, you can quickly change to a different range of typefaces and sizes. The time needed to respecify the type for this chapter and have the computer show the new font was about thirty seconds.

The fourth step on the graph is prepping the photos. You now do that with a ruler, proportion wheel, and photostat camera. With a graphics computer, you'll place the photos in a scanner, scan them, and save them in a file to be incorporated into the layout. You'll still need to mark the percentage of enlargement or reduction on them before you ship the mechanicals, but you can play with the photo sizing and cropping right up until the time you save the file for the service bureau. And if the layout changes, there won't be any need to make new photostats.

Traditionally, the last step—making mechanicals—involves an art table, T-square, triangles, waxer, galley type, and so on. For some projects, you may want to prepare a traditional mechanical, but most jobs—including four-color process jobs with overlays—can be done from start to finish on the computer.

The net result of these changes is that, while the designer who worked on the brochure without a graphics computer divided his time between a number of different tasks and tools, of the ten hours spent working on the job by the designer who used a computer, about four and a

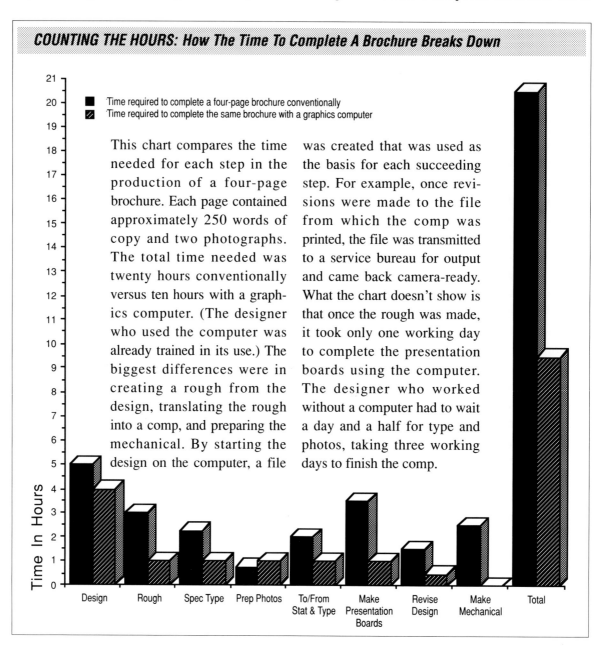

**COUNTING THE HOURS: How The Time To Complete A Brochure Breaks Down**

■ Time required to complete a four-page brochure conventionally
▨ Time required to complete the same brochure with a graphics computer

This chart compares the time needed for each step in the production of a four-page brochure. Each page contained approximately 250 words of copy and two photographs. The total time needed was twenty hours conventionally versus ten hours with a graphics computer. (The designer who used the computer was already trained in its use.) The biggest differences were in creating a rough from the design, translating the rough into a comp, and preparing the mechanical. By starting the design on the computer, a file was created that was used as the basis for each succeeding step. For example, once revisions were made to the file from which the comp was printed, the file was transmitted to a service bureau for output and came back camera-ready. What the chart doesn't show is that once the rough was made, it took only one working day to complete the presentation boards using the computer. The designer who worked without a computer had to wait a day and a half for type and photos, taking three working days to finish the comp.

Time In Hours

Design | Rough | Spec Type | Prep Photos | To/From Stat & Type | Make Presentation Boards | Revise Design | Make Mechanical | Total half hours were spent sitting in front of a computer monitor.

### Getting Into Training

It's one thing to imagine yourself sitting in front of a screen, spinning logos, and splashing color hither and yon. It's quite another to acquire the skills needed to do so with the greatest of ease.

Before deciding to buy into the notion of a digital studio, you have to buy into the notion that you're actually going to learn to use the gear to its full potential. In some circumstances, you may be able to justify the cost of a graphics computer without fully integrating it into your studio. However, what's the sense of buying and installing such a tool if you don't intend to take full advantage of its capabilities?

There's a definite learning curve, just like there was when you learned to use a technical pen. The good news is that, especially in the beginning, most designers find they spend most of their computer time with just one or two core programs, usually a page-layout program or a drawing program. That limits the number of command sequences you have to remember and the number of pages of software manuals you need to read.

For some people, the changeover to a graphics computer is easy and natural; others find it takes a little bit of effort. Either way, if you're committed to making the change, the knowledge and the skills will follow.

You may also consider hiring a skilled computer graphics consultant or an artist from another studio to train you and your staff for a few hours each week. This kind of one-to-one help can save hours of frustration. Hiring someone to give you a quick orientation to an unfamiliar software package makes good economic sense, will make you more comfortable with the equipment more quickly, and will minimize the amount of "downtime" you will inevitably have if you rely solely on trial and error to learn.

The section on page 121 discusses training alternatives and the costs of training time (whether self-inflicted or purchased outside). Remember to figure in lost productivity and the cost of training when assessing the true costs of adding computers to your studio.

### Mac Vs. Big Blue: Is There A Difference?

Apple Computer made a very wise decision when it created the Macintosh. In the face of overwhelming criticism from software developers, Apple wrote very strict guidelines for Macintosh software. Their goal was to have all Macintosh programs use the same basic command sets (i.e. Command-S would be "save file" for all programs instead of having some programs implement "save file" as Command-E or some other nonsensical combination). Despite the squawking, many developers went along with the scheme. The result has been that it's possible to launch a Macintosh program you've never seen before and already know how to open, save, and print a file. In addition, Macintosh programs tend to operate in ways that are standardized. There's a built-in knowledge base as you move from program to program. That dramatically cuts the time needed to learn the rudiments of new programs. It also reduces the frustration factor: Spending an hour or two trying to make a new software program print a document when you have a deadline hanging over your head is simply maddening.

Graphics software for IBM and IBM-compatible machines varies wildly in terms of difficulty of learning. Some programs are as simple to learn as the average Macintosh program. Others are incredibly complex, the creations of programmers who evidently believe that graphic artists have nothing better to do with their time than to disassemble the programming code in order to figure out how to use the software.

The bottom line is, if you intend to standardize on IBM-compatible machines, plan on more formal and time-consuming training.

How much time you need for training and how quickly you assimilate the computer into your routine will vary according to your affinity for machines. The good news is that the computer allows you to make this transition at your own pace. Because we had both operated dedicated typesetters and already owned two IBM-compatible computers, we started doing page layouts on our Macintosh immediately. Within an hour of opening the boxes, we were printing out our first simple layout. Others suggest going slower. Will Hopkins of the Will Hopkins Group in New York City began by writing correspondence on the firm's Macintosh. As he felt better about the computer, he began doing design work on it.

The time needed to become proficient with a program will vary also. After three weeks of using Quark XPress® every day, we felt we were being productive, and that our lack of knowledge about the program wasn't slowing us down. After six months, again using the program almost every day, we had learned most of the nuances of the software. Adobe Illustrator® and Aldus Freehand® take longer to master. While designers report they are able to do useful work in these programs with a few days practice, it can take a year of constant use to truly master the many features they offer. Especially with page layout programs, a solid working knowledge of mechanical production and the printing process are more important than technical knowledge about computers.

### Attack Of The Dreaded Tech-Heads

No one knows your business or your clients as well as you do. There's no one set of standard operating procedures, no one set of hardware and software, that fit everyone.

That means you'll either have to learn enough about graphics computers to be your own technical advisor, have someone in your studio become one, or hire an outside consultant. Your local computer dealer is probably not the place to get advice on print production techniques. There are, however, a lot of Macintosh users just like you who are eager to share techniques and discoveries. Users groups have formed in most major cities and universities. Join one. Your service bureau can be a valuable source of information. If the folks at the bureau are adventurous and skilled with the equipment, they are usually happy to help you solve problems, discuss the merits of competing software packages, and swap operating tips.

### What Jobs Will You Automate?

So, you've decided you want a graphics computer and you're willing to commit yourself to some training and to learning about the hardware and software. There's still the question of what functions you choose to automate. In the beginning, your graphics computer will do more to save you money on the cost of outside materials and photostats and speed the flow of work through the studio than it will to save man-hours. But there are at least two ways you can reduce the man-hours spent on a job with a graphics computer.

***Remove steps from the process by integrating them.*** In our case, we design the format for most publications before we begin writing. We then write directly into the file that contains our rough design. This eliminates the problems of copyfitting and of editing and rerunning type to fit a layout. Similarly, if you place the actual copy on your presentation boards, you may find you can get the client to make all copy revisions at that point, omitting a re-proof between revision and mechanicals.

*Get the project into the computer at the earliest possible stage* and eliminate work done manually. The files you send to the service bureau should come back camera-ready. With enough skill, just about anything you can do traditionally (with the exception of certain airbrush techniques and the use of fonts not yet available) can be done on a graphics computer. Because the electronic files reduce the time spent creating materials at each succeeding stage of a project, the earlier in a project you begin working with the computer, the less time will be spent recreating materials. If an electronic file can be sent to the service bureau so that it comes back ready to ship to the printer, you will save time in assembling the final mechanical art.

---

## Getting Up To Speed: Which Tasks Should You Automate First?

Most artists find they start out by automating simple tasks, then do more of their work at the screen as they gain proficiency. Knowing what to try using a computer for and what's better done by hand is a skill that develops as you learn what your computer can do. The steps marked ❶ are easy and most artists can perform them within a month of buying a computer. The ones marked ❷ require skills that develop more slowly. When it comes to conceptual design, most artists say a sketch pad is faster and freer than using a computer to create thumbnails.

❶ *Roughs:* Graphics computers are ideally suited to producing roughs, trying a variety of typefaces. The use of a laser printer allows you to quickly see your choices.

❶ *Setting/specifying type:* Unless you have to enter long blocks of copy, the computer is a quick way to see and set type.

❶ *Making position photos:* It's easy to scan photos and import them into a layout or use them as the basis for an illustration. However, you may find that using a photocopier is faster until you get up to speed using a scanner. If you use a lot of position images, we recommend switching as quickly as possible, though.

❷ *Designing logos/headlines:* The software needed to produce the broad range of effects most artists desire takes time to learn. Plan to work into this phase over three months. Plan to spend some non-productive time learning the programs, too.

❶/❷ *Presentation boards:* Doing a full-color comp strictly on a computer for jobs that require photos, illustrations, and screens requires three to five software packages and experience with color laser printers. However, the base materials for a comp—type, headlines, photo boxes—can be created with just a page layout program. You can make very nice comps by printing these on an imagesetter, pasting color photocopies into the photo boxes, and laying tint screens. As you gain experience, try using a color scanner and color printer to print comps in color.

❶/❷ *Making camera-ready mechanicals:* Until you're scanning and making line illustrations, you won't be able to produce files that can be printed on an imagesetter as final camera-ready mechanicals. First, try using the computer to produce your type in place with photo boxes. As you get more experience, you can add position images.

# Chapter Four:
# Costs, Benefits, And Cautions

**Real Costs, Real Benefits**

**Real Costs: One Studio's Experience**

**Help Where It Hurts The Most: Production**

**Profit Opportunities And A Final Warning**

**Buyer Beware: Tales From The Dark Side**

# Real Costs, Real Benefits

After reading the last chapter, you may be asking yourself if adding computers to your studio is really worth the disruption, downtime, and expense.

The answer, according to those who have, is an unequivocal yes. While some of that enthusiasm is created by the expanded capabilities computers add, most say increased profit is the most important benefit.

Graphics computers can increase your profit in two ways: By increasing productivity—getting more projects out the door per manhour—and by lowering expenses.

Before deciding if you need a graphics computer and how much you should spend on equipment, you should weigh the foreseeable costs and benefits.

## What Do Mechanicals Really Cost?

You can expect outside expenses for type, photostats, and mechanical boards to drop if you get a graphics computer installed and operating. If you can use typestyles available on the computer for headlines, you'll save on press type as well. If you currently have someone taking type to the typesetter or dropping off stats, there may be some labor saved, too.

To make a comparison, you'll need to know what your true costs are for a typical job. When adding it up, be realistic. Get out the invoices for a job and see what the real expenses were. Remember to add the cost of rerunning type that wasn't specified correctly and rush charges for type or stats needed to make revisions requested by the client.

## Comparing Costs

The four-page brochure used as a test of total time spent to complete a project on page 54 was also used to compare costs in a traditional studio versus a digital studio.

| | | Without Computer | With Computer |
|---|---|---|---|
| Design | (@ $65/hr.) | $ 325 | $ 260 |
| Rough | (@ $65/hr.) | 195 | 65 |
| Mark up copy | (@ $15/hr.) | 30 | — |
| Prep (or scan) photos | (@ $15/hr.) | 13 | 15 |
| To/from stat & type | (@ $15/hr.) | 30 | 15 |
| Make presentation boards | (@ $65/hr.) | 228 | 65 |
| Revise design | (@ $65/hr.) | 98 | 38 |
| Prep file for typesetter | (@ $65/hr.) | — | 38 |
| Make mechanical | (@ $15/hr.) | 30 | — |
| Mark for printer | (@ $65/hr.) | 98 | 49 |
| | | | |
| Type | | 175 | 28 |
| Photostats | | 25 | — |
| Materials | | 23 | 4 |
| | | | |
| TOTAL: | | $ 1270 | $ 577 |

### Labor-Saving or Labor-Intensive?

In the chart on the preceding page, you can see that working with a graphics computer eliminates copy mark-up and making mechanicals. On the whole, computers *do* save man-hours. More importantly, they automate wearisome chores, freeing up time that can be spent on the creative aspects of the business. These time savings probably won't materialize for three to six months after installation; they'll show up once you're able to operate your core software programs from memory.

The form in which clients submit copy is a small hurdle for many studios. If your clients submit copy in manuscript form, you—as the typesetter—now have to enter the text and learn how to manipulate it. Some designers hire a word processor on a freelance basis to enter text. Some use OCR (optical copy recognition) software and a scanner to convert typed copy directly into computer text. When it was first introduced for desktop computers, OCR software was not terribly accurate and a bit cumbersome to use. By 1990, packages had been improved to the point that a program costing $750-$1,000 would capture *typed* text with fewer errors than the average typesetter would make in rekeying it. Also, since most businesses use desktop computers for word processing, many studios ask clients to submit copy on disk. Using inexpensive software, the copy on the client's disk is converted to a text file that is then placed in a layout. Even if your clients use IBM-compatible computers and you buy an Apple Macintosh, you can convert their files for your use.

Revisions to projects can be made much more quickly—and at far less expense—with a graphics computer. Look at the chart at left. What if the client decided he wanted a serif instead of a sans-serif face after you'd already completed mechanicals? Working traditionally, you'd need to re-mark the manuscript, rerun the type, and paste the new type on the mechanicals. At a minimum, the cost to you of these alterations would be $60 in labor fees and perhaps $100 in new type charges. With a graphics computer, you'd spend $40 in labor (to change the specs in your page layout file and get it to the typesetter) and $30 for the new type.

One of the biggest payoffs is in the shortening of throughput time—the number of days that elapse between the time you begin a job and the time you deliver it. You can scan photos instead of sending out for photostats and waiting for their return. When making presentation boards, most studios use type from their laser printer, rather than sending out for typeset copy. Unless you want a face that's not available yet for graphics computers, there's no need to go to the art supply store for press type; even if you keep a big stock of press type on hand, it's much faster to simply type in a headline and space, condense, expand, or kern it than it is to press it out, stat it, and then use a knife to fit it to the layout. Most service bureaus that convert computer files to typeset output give twenty-four hour turnaround as standard service. Once the files are returned from the bureau, they're mechanicals, ready to mark and ship.

### Saving Days

The net result of these savings is that the designer who used a computer to work on the brochure began designing on Monday, presented the comp Wednesday morning, got approval on Thursday, and delivered mechanicals Friday afternoon. The designer who worked without a computer started on Monday, but couldn't show a comp until Friday. He got approval the following Monday, sent corrections that afternoon, and delivered mechanicals Wednesday. The computer helps clear projects off your docket and shortens the interval between selling a job and billing it.

## Real Costs: One Studio's Experience

In 1986, TLI, a West Coast graphics firm, was doing okay. The firm had revenues of $871,000 and seven designers industriously bent over their art tables. With relatively low costs for outside type and photostats of about $47,000 and billings per designer of $97,000, president Tom Lewis was pleased with his profit picture.

In 1987 something remarkable happened. Lewis decided to buy a Macintosh. Just one. He bought the computer as an experiment, more to see what it would do than with any master plan in mind.

What the Macintosh did was turn the studio on its ear organizationally. Over the course of the next two years billings per designer leaped 30 percent, while the staff got smaller and costs plummeted. With payroll and expenses down, profits shot up. Tom Lewis became a true believer.

"It seems that every time we bought a Mac, a few months later, someone left," Lewis told fellow designers at a recent computer graphics conference. "We didn't plan it that way, but that's what happened." One of the designers who left was unhappy with the way work had been reorganized in the shop after the installation of the Macintosh system. Another just felt he would be happier elsewhere.

Lewis readily acknowledged that having designers become unhappy and leave is a very real cost to his firm; a cost that is at least partially linked to the arrival of the graphics computers. But he also feels very strongly that the economic benefits outweigh the effort required to recruit and integrate new designers.

While the cost side of the equation was important, there were noticeable gains in productivity, as shown by the increase in billings per designer.

Lewis believes that's due to a decrease in downtime. Instead of picking up a job, working to the point where type or stats are needed, prepping those materials, and then moving on to another project while the type house does its work, his staff is now able to keep working on a project from roughs right through to presentation materials without stopping. The fewer times a designer has to stop and restart a job, the better.

The economics, Lewis insists, are only part of the picture. The arrival of the computers also coincided with a renewed vigor in the studio. "The computer challenged and energized the staff, and I think that's as much responsible for the increase in our billings as anything. I think our clients saw that new energy in our work," he says. Clients like enthusiastic design firms, and that made Lewis's job easier.

There have been other changes. Lewis says the computers have made his designers very intense about their work: "I used to walk into the office and people would look up and chat with me. Now they hardly know I'm there."

Despite the intensity of their concentration, the designers have developed a strong network, and Lewis encourages them to show their work to each other and talk frequently.

Lewis emits a painful chuckle when he says that the computer "has us by the throat. I wouldn't buy more black and white systems. The systems we buy in the future will be color. We want to stay on the leading edge of this technology."

Still, there's no question in Lewis's mind about returning to manual design. An iconoclast when it comes to basic training, Lewis won't even hire a designer who hasn't had at least some Macintosh experience: "It isn't my job to teach them the tools of their trade."

This sentiment certainly isn't the mainstream approach today—many studios provide formal and informal training—but then, Tom Lewis may just be a sign of things to come.

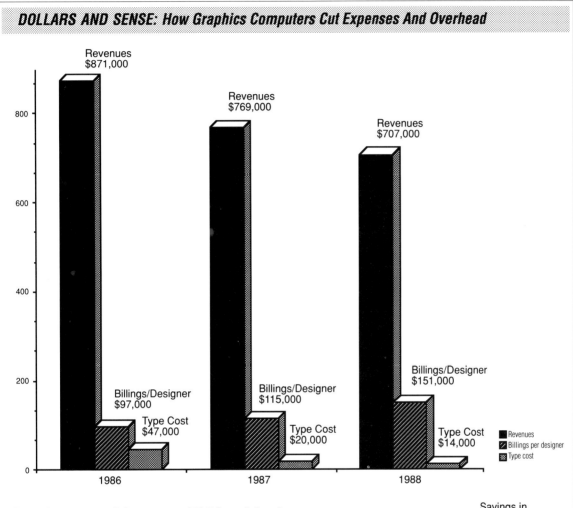

Over the course of three years, TLI found that its billings per designer jumped 30 percent. In 1986, the company had no graphics computers; in 1987, it had one, and in 1988, three. At the same time, staff declined from seven designers to five and the cost of type from outside suppliers dropped by 60 percent. The graph at right compares the cost of the computers purchased to the money saved on type and photostats during 1987 and 1988. The firm spent $33,000 on its computers while it saved $60,000 on its type and photostat costs during that same period. The amounts shown on the left side of the graphs are in thousands of dollars.

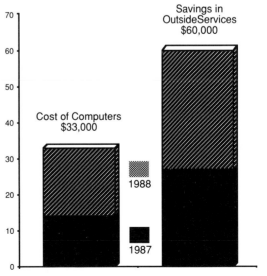

## Help Where It Hurts The Most: Production

Financially, a graphics computer helps designers most—and most immediately—in the production of mechanicals. Learning graphics software and learning to adapt your design process to the computer will take a few months, but you can start laying out pages and setting type almost as quickly as you can get the machine screwed together. Also, it's easy to put a dollar figure on the cost of type and labor for mechanicals, so you're likely to notice savings there first. As you learn the computer and begin to improvise new ways to use it in your studio, you'll likely find that it enhances your capability—making bigger or more complex projects feasible and profitable—and that it allows you to give better service to your clients in the form of more complete presentations and shorter turnaround times.

Investments that pay for themselves immediately in reduced costs are unusual in business. In our case, the amount of money the computer saved on type and photostats was enough to justify our investment. Other designers, especially those with a high volume of mechanical production, say the cost of owning a system is more than covered by their savings on type alone.

To determine whether a graphics computer will raise your total monthly expenses or lower them, you need to calculate a couple of basic numbers.

Typesetters traditionally charge per galley of type. When you send electronic mechanicals to a service bureau for typeset output, however, you'll pay per finished page (unless you submit your electronic files as galley type and paste them up manually).

Figure your current type cost per page of finished mechanicals. In the case of the four-page brochure illustrated earlier, the per-page cost of type set traditionally was $46.50 ($175 for galley type plus $11 for press type).

A graphics computer system that will allow

---

### EAR OF BAT, EYE OF NEWT: The Other Stuff You Need Costs Money Too

You already know that nothing (with the possible exception of bubble gum) works as simply as its promoters claim. In addition to hardware, software, training, and patience, you'll need supplies to operate a computer graphics system. While not exorbitant, their cost should be part of your calculations. Use these numbers as a rough guide until you can pinpoint your actual costs:

*Laser prints................................$ 0.10/each*
Includes the cost of a laser printer amortized over its life cycle, cost of toner and cost of paper. Figure you'll print each page five times before it's ready to send to the service bureau for typeset output.

*Disks to store/transport files......$ 0.15/page*
Disks cost approximately $1.20 each. You can store three finished mechanicals with scans on each disk and reuse them until they wear out or you need them for archival storage (three reuse cycles per disk).

*Art materials..............................$0.50/page*
Although your need for press type, mechanical board, and rubylith will drop precipitously, you'll still need *some*.

*Total..........$ 1.15/finished mechanical page*
Add $1.15 to your cost of type per finished page to get the base materials cost for your electronic mechanicals.

you to design and produce complex mechanicals will cost about $12,000 at 1990 prices. If you finance the system, your equipment cost will be about $415 per month (thirty-six months at 15 percent interest). You can expect to pay between $7 and $10 per page for typeset output from your electronic files on RC paper or $14 per sheet for film. Obviously, the more pages you produce each month, the lower your total per-page cost. In addition to the cost of type, there

## WHERE THE BOTTOM LINE MEETS THE COST-CURVE: Will A Computer Save You Money?

These figures show how the cost of buying type from typesetters balances against the cost of operating a graphics computer system for one small studio. *Your costs may be different.* The comparison is based on a computer system cost of $12,000 (leased at $415 per month), type from electronic files at $10 per page, and supply expense of $1.15 per finished page versus an average cost per finished mechanical of $46.50 for traditionally set galley type. For this studio the break-even point—where the costs of operating the graphics computer equal the cost of traditionally set type—is only twelve finished mechanicals per month. At higher volumes, the graphics computer actually saves the studio money each month.

| Pages Per Month | Using A Graphics Computer | | Traditional Typesetting | | |
| --- | --- | --- | --- | --- | --- |
| | Per Page | Total/Month | Per Page | Total/Month | Net Savings |
| 10 | $ 52.00 | $ 520.00 | $ 46.50 | $ 465.00 | $ (-55.00) |
| 15 | 38.17 | 572.50 | 46.50 | 697.50 | 125.00 |
| 20 | 31.25 | 625.00 | 46.50 | 930.00 | 305.00 |
| 25 | 27.10 | 677.50 | 46.50 | 1,162.50 | 485.00 |
| 30 | 24.33 | 730.00 | 46.50 | 1,395.00 | 665.00 |
| 35 | 22.36 | 782.50 | 46.50 | 1,627.50 | 845.00 |
| 40 | 20.88 | 835.00 | 46.50 | 1,860.00 | 1,025.00 |
| 45 | 19.72 | 887.50 | 46.50 | 2,092.50 | 1,205.00 |
| 50 | 18.80 | 940.00 | 46.50 | 2,325.00 | 1,385.00 |
| 55 | 18.05 | 992.50 | 46.50 | 2,557.50 | 1,565.00 |
| 60 | 17.42 | 1,045.00 | 46.50 | 2790.00 | 1,745.00 |
| 65 | 16.88 | 1,097.50 | 46.50 | 3,022.50 | 1,925.00 |
| 70 | 16.43 | 1,150.00 | 46.50 | 3,255.00 | 2,105.00 |
| 75 | 16.03 | 1,202.50 | 46.50 | 3,487.50 | 2,285.00 |
| 80 | 15.69 | 1,255.00 | 46.50 | 3,720.00 | 2,465.00 |
| 85 | 15.38 | 1,307.50 | 46.50 | 3,952.50 | 2,645.00 |
| 90 | 15.11 | 1,360.00 | 46.50 | 4,185.00 | 2,825.00 |
| 95 | 14.87 | 1,412.50 | 46.50 | 4,417.50 | 3,005.00 |
| 100 | 14.65 | 1,465.00 | 46.50 | 4,650.00 | 3,185.00 |
| 125 | 13.82 | 1,727.50 | 46.50 | 5,812.50 | 4,085.00 |
| 150 | 13.27 | 1,990.00 | 46.50 | 6,975.00 | 4,985.00 |

are some other costs (for paper, laser prints, and so on). Adding up the cost of the equipment and supplies (but *not including the cost of labor*) using the graphics system for finished mechanicals (not just galley type) would result in per page costs as shown in the table on the preceding page.

These figures were calculated using $10 as the cost for setting the electronic files, plus $1.15 per finished mechanical for supplies, plus the monthly cost of the equipment, divided by the total number of pages. If you set more than thirty finished pages a month, you should be able to buy RC paper output from a service bureau for $8 per page; even less if you have an extraordinarily high volume.

Labor costs aren't included in the table because they depend on how fast you (or the computer operators) are and how much you pay yourself or your designers. For straight layout using the computer, we've found that ten finished pages per day is about as fast as you're likely to get. This includes fitting type and photos to a reasonably complex rough layout, sizing and marking photos, and checking the file to ensure it's ready for the service bureau. This figure *doesn't* include design time or the time needed to scan the photos (allow five minutes per photo if you're fast, eight minutes if you're not). At the time of publication, a quick survey of desktop publishers in the New York area showed that the average *billing* rate for computer layout work was $65 per hour.

For many studios it's possible to recoup the cost of a full-featured graphics computer system out of the money saved on type and photostats. Once the gear is paid for, your profit margin grows. You don't have to tell your clients that your costs have dropped and productivity is up unless you choose to. Stop grinning. Keep your eye on the market and readjust your pricing as needed; even if your clients don't know costs are

down, your competitors surely will. Some design firms will choose to cut prices rather than increase profits with the savings they realize from installing a graphics computer.

### Color Yourself Green

Obviously, the graphics computer didn't print out money for you to pay for it with. The money came from somewhere: It came out of the cash you would have otherwise sent to your typesetter. You have, in essence, transferred profit from the typesetting company to your business.

Another area with a similarly potent profit potential is in doing color pre-press work on a graphics computer.

*Spot Color:* Spot color tints using single-color Pantone® screens or mixtures of cyan, magenta, yellow, and black can be created easily using many of the major page layout or illustration software packages.

Quark XPress®, for example, lets you pick colors for your screens by typing in a PMS® number, specifying screen densities numerically, or using the mouse to pick a color from a color wheel. The software automatically figures screen angles and densities, and, when the file is printed on an imagesetter, two, three, or four negative films are automatically created.

You'll pay more for the film than for a single sheet mechanical on paper (about $14 per piece, or $64 for a four-color page), but you save the cost of the camera work and stripping. In a piece with a number of tint blocks, the savings can be considerable. Again, you choose how much of the savings to pass along to your clients.

*Photographic Color:* Before you protest too loudly, look at Lance Hidy's *Temple*, reproduced on page 17. The original was scanned and separatd using desktop equipment.

Color pre-press from the desktop is a reality (see *Color From The Desktop*, page 154 for the technical details). At the time of publication, magazine-quality continuous-tone color separations (such as photographs) were being done on desktop graphics computers by an adventurous few. As the links between high-end separation systems such as Scitex, Hell, and Crosfield improve, expect the price, availability, and quality of desktop separations to improve quickly. How much profit could you build into a color brochure if you could get single-page composite film output from your computer files for $175 per page—regardless of the number of individual separations—instead of paying $75 per separation plus the stripping charge?

How much easier would your work become if you could scan in color artwork—magazine photos, transparencies, illustrations—combine them in a page layout, and use that as a presentation comp? Would you like to be able to crop and position photos precisely on your computer so that the strippers don't get a chance to have an opinion about where they should go?

## Doesn't This Silver Lining Have A Cloud?

You bet it does. Things happen. Things like software mutating in the night and files evaporating into thin air. Computers are pretty complex gizmos. Their propensity to indulge in capricious behavior is legendary. We've all heard at least one apocryphal story about a computer that ruined someone's life by billing them a dime for something they didn't buy and then refusing to credit their account.

Our own corollary to Murphy's Law states that the more wonderful the technology, the more likely it is to experience catastrophic failure. These failures tend to occur when you're facing a deadline. After all, you use the gear most when you have a project to complete quickly, right? If the project is sufficiently important to your health, well-being, and general

sanity, you can count on the failure occurring on a holiday weekend when there isn't another technically-competent soul in this hemisphere who's anywhere near a telephone.

Some of the uglier manifestations of this corollary include:

*USEs* (Unexpected Software Events): This is the software package that has performed brilliantly up until the very moment you push the button to print the client's proofs of a forty-eight page annual report. Preventives for this include backing up your work faithfully and scrupulously guarding the integrity of the master disks of the programs you use most frequently.

*New Software Syndrome:* Never, ever, *ever* rely on a new software package to complete a project at the last minute—not even if your best friend has had the program for months and won't stop raving about it. The variety of possible configurations of hardware and software is infinite; therefore, so is the number of things that can go wrong.

Even if your friend's hardware and software are identical to yours, you could still have a problem. We have two Mac IIs with absolutely stone solid identical hardware, system files, and software. For about three months, one of the machines refused to print Optima to our laser printer. Copying the Optima files from the functioning machine to the non-functioning one didn't help. Neither did switching the hard disks containing the fonts and software. One day the recalcitrant computer just up and started printing Optima again and has done so ever since.

One of our fondest memories involves the release of a new Apple system file (version 6.0) for the Macintosh.

In its literature, Apple encourages users of its equipment to change their system software as soon as a new version becomes available. As good corporate citizens, we eagerly obtained a copy of this new software the week after Apple released it. At the same time, we added a new utility package and some fonts. Almost immediately, all of the computers in the studio began spontaneously freezing up, usually just as a mechanical was completed and ready to print.

We suspected a virus. Several laborious hours later, every file on every hard disk had been checked. The machines weren't infected.

We suspected one of the new utility packages. It was removed from the hard drives. More freezing and data loss followed.

We suspected the fonts. They were removed, with the same results.

When the problems continued, there was only one suspect still in the running: Apple's new system software. As Arthur Conan Doyle's character Sherlock Holmes noted some years ago, when all solutions but one have been eliminated, the only solution left, however improbable, must be correct.

When we switched back to the previous version of the system file, the problems disappeared. Total downtime: Two days. Frustration factor: Extremely high. Two weeks later, Apple released an update for System 6.0 and admitted the software was a bit "buggy."

This disaster struck just ten days before final materials were due for a job that made up almost twenty percent of our studio's revenues that year. The adage about not changing horses in mid-stream applies. If your system is working, be very cautious in your tinkering. If you're involved in a big project, don't tinker at all.

Also, test all new software by using it to create a print file, then send that file to your service bureau to make sure *their* equipment doesn't have a problem with it.

***Temporary CPU Confusion:*** Until we began using computers, we, too, subscribed to the notion of computers as all-knowing and logical (as opposed to being prone to memory lapses and inexplicable behavior, like your senile uncle

Albert). Wrong. Your computer *will* get confused from time to time for no apparent reason. If you had to shuffle five decks of cards at once, it's likely you'd drop a few, too. The difficulties may well prove to be immune to deductive reasoning: For example, scrolling through layout files with grayscale photographs in them frequently makes one of our Macs freeze up, but the others never do.

To prevent damage to your sanity, save your files frequently. Then, when the machine hangs and refuses to respond to vigorous pounding on the keyboard and a round of connector-jiggling, you can switch it off and back on again. This is the digital equivalent of death and reincarnation with the ever-popular bonus of remembering the details of past lives (your data, which you had previously saved and backed up).

***Disk Crash:*** Hard disks do sometimes "go south," responding to your pleading with a dumb, blank stare: "Illustration? What illustration?" Sometimes it's just a piece of a file that disappears. Once every two years or so, it's every blessed thing on your hard disk (work in progress, funny sounds collected from friends, accounts receivable, client lists, and other mundane, but critical, data). Back up your data files.

Floppy disks are more prone to failure than hard disks, so backing up data on them is a calculated risk. The odds that both a hard disk *and* the floppies containing the copies will go bad simultaneously is small. We hope. Some gurus recommend tape back ups, others swear by redundant hard drives.

***Hardware Failure:*** Sometimes the beasts just quit. Fortunately, our survey (not a scientific one by any means) indicates that equipment failure is infrequent. In three years, we lost two logic boards (sort of a computerized cardiac arrest), one power supply, and a CRT (monitor tube). Any of these events can be mighty inconvenient if you don't have a back-up plan. Buy one more workstation than you think you need, check whether your local computer dealer has used gear for rent in a crisis, and/or make friends with folks who have extra equipment you can borrow for a week or so in an emergency.

*Idiot Time:* All software packages require some training time and some are almost fiendishly difficult to master. For the first six months, figure your output of finished pages at about half the maximum rate—five pages a day for straight layout and production; less if the job involves tricky overlays or other things that go beyond the basics of cut, paste, and move.

Any time you move to a new level of complexity—adding a new kind of software package or going from basic to advanced features in a familiar program—add some hours to your schedule. You'll need them to get a firm grasp on the new commands, file structures, and sequence of actions required.

## Cost Effective?

The time and labor needed to rectify the above situations has to be deducted from your workday. When calculating the benefits of owning a graphics computer, don't blithely assume you're immune. If you do, you're sure to get snakebit. You'll survive, of course, and the computer will still be a good deal for your business, but the sense of serenity (hubris?) that comes with technical competence will take longer to attain.

## Yes, But I Want The Money!

The foregoing is just another way of saying, "No pain, no gain." The pain is real, but so is the potential for expanding your business and increasing profits.

Fortunately, the pain is episodic while the boosts in productivity and the freedom from some of the more onerous chores associated with

this business can be enjoyed every day. If you want the extra profits, the instant access to fonts, illustrations, stats, and special effects, you can learn to live with the foibles of hardware manufacturers, the follies of software developers, and the inevitable breakdowns. It's far from a continuing nightmare and there are plenty of computer compadres out there to commiserate with. After a while, you may even develop a sense of humor about losing an illustration file that took two hours to create.

Hopefully the first section of this book has given you a realistic picture of what to expect—good and bad—and a yardstick to judge your own studio by. Use the charts as a guide, not as gospel. Your costs may be vastly different. You may have a typesetter who charges peon's rates for galleys. You may do a lot of design and very little production. In that case, you may have to delve a little deeper, looking to expanded capabilities or higher productivity for the justification to make the investment.

Ready or not, like it or not, digital design is upon us. Ask yourself where your business will be in five years. If the answer is, "Still profitable without a computer in the joint," read no further. Our purpose is to help you make an *informed* choice about computers, not sell you equipment.

If, on the other hand, you're ready to embrace the new order (before it runs over you), read on.

Before running to the nearest computer dealer and exposing your checkbook to the ravages of an underinformed salesperson, you owe it to yourself to figure out exactly what *kind* of system makes sense—financially and professionally—for your studio.

Deciding to purchase a graphics computer is tough enough; hacking your way through the tangle of promotional hype is even tougher. Fortunately, others have been there before you. In the next section. we'll look at ways to get a handle on what you do—and *don't*—need.

# Section II:
# What Should I Buy?

**73** Chapter Five:
How To Buy—Researching And Reading

**81** Chapter Six:
Hardware Wars

**91** Chapter Seven:
Building A Shopping List

**107** Chapter Eight:
Ante Up—How To Pay The Piper

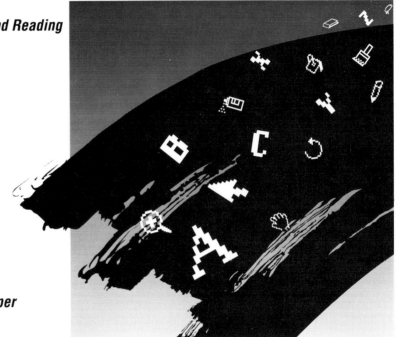

# Chapter Five:
# How To Buy—Research And Reading

**Getting The Straight Story:**
**You Hear It Through The Grapevine**

**Read 'Em And Weep:**
**What The Magazines Don't Tell You**

**Manufacturer's (Mis)Information**

**To Market To Market: Where To Buy**

If you like to shop, you'll love this chapter. We could have cut the length of this book to ten pages by simply telling you that you definitely need a computer and printing a shopping list for you to follow–but that would have taken all the fun out of it. By investing in a graphics computer, you're going to enter a whole new world. You'll have to learn a new language and figure out the customs of the natives. Most designers say the discoveries, the adventure, and the profits justify the effort. Fortunately, you won't have to make the trip alone. Unfortunately, there's no friendly AAA travel service to give you a road map, either.

There is no *Consumer Reports* for computer graphics; no cool voice of reason that cuts through the promotional hype, hysteria, and general miasma of misinformation that surrounds the subject. That puts the responsibility for making an intelligent purchase squarely on your shoulders.

There are two ways to deal with this. You can hire a consultant or you can figure it out for yourself.

Many designers choose to go it alone, investing their time in learning about graphics computers instead of investing money in outside expertise. A few studios combined these approaches, with the owners learning a little and leaning on an outsider for the rest.

The studios who have hired an outsider to help them report that they made the changeover with less downtime and less frustration than most of those who went it alone. They also said that they were able to more fully integrate the computer into their work flow and reap the economic benefits more quickly (thus recouping their investment faster) by having an experienced consultant help. All of them said that the benefits they realized far outweighed the consultant's fees. Our own experience in helping set up computer systems for other studios confirms this: We see them doing more work with the computers, doing it more quickly and with more professional results, and having less frustration after a few sessions. There are many things that can be demonstrated in ten minutes that take an hour or more to glean from a software manual. There are also specific procedures—for saving files and transmitting them to a service bureau, in specifying spot color screens, in building page layout files—that aren't covered in any manual.

## These Hands For Hire

Most established computer consultants are experts in DOS machines. Unless you're buying an IBM or compatible, the first requirement for a consultant for a design studio is that they know the Macintosh intimately. Ask if they are designers and how many projects they have actually produced using a computer. Your best bet is to find a designer who has heavy Macintosh experience. Ask the consultant to demonstrate the gear for you *before* you buy his time. During the demo ask questions about color, graphics, illustration programs, and printing to an imagesetter. You'll quickly get a feeling whether the consultant's knowledge is book knowledge or the result of practical experience.

Computer dealerships are not a great place to find consultants. Some dealers—not many—employ designers to sell graphics computers and assist their customers.

When you begin seriously thinking about buying equipment, join your local users group. Unless you live in Hot Coffee, Mississippi, or some similarly isolated rural community, there is a users group devoted to computers near you. Universities are always a good place to inquire about users groups. It's likely that someone in the group will either be qualified to advise you on equipment options and sources or will know someone who is.

74

## Dealer's Choice

We haven't said many good things about computer dealers so far. That's partly because we haven't gotten much valuable information from dealers. We also tend toward weighing the options for ourselves without the help of a dealer who has an obvious financial stake in our decision. It's not that dealers are dishonest. Our experience, and that of other studios, has been that the number of dealers who truly understand the design business and the needs of design studios is small. You may be lucky. There may be a dealer near you who has designers on staff; designers who have direct, day-to-day experience with the hardware and software you're considering buying. If so, take full advantage of their expertise. But don't count on getting it.

In the larger world of number crunching and computer sales, there are dealers who assemble turnkey hardware/software packages for specific purposes. These dealers are called Value Added Re-sellers (VARs). While some VARs do sell graphic arts equipment, as of this writing, we weren't aware of any VARs devoted solely to graphics computers and the design studio market.

This means that the quality of the advice and service you receive from the dealer is purely a matter of pot luck.

## With A Little Help From Your Friends

A majority of the designers we spoke with said they flew solo—no consultant, no dealer help—on their decisions about hardware and software. The majority of these also said they asked for and received good advice from other designers who already had graphics computers. It's just like those Tarzan movies where information travels from tribe to tribe via signal drums. There's a well-established grapevine that connects service bureaus, design studios, and graphics "hackers" (programmers and hobbyists).

Information about products, solutions to common problems, software reviews, and even computer viruses travel through it into studios across the U.S. It even bridges the oceans, as firms with international connections exchange information with overseas contacts.

Whether or not you have a consultant help you with your initial purchase, this grapevine will be your primary source of information on how to use your computers most effectively, on new software, for problem-solving advice, and for general moral support. The sooner you tap into it, the sooner you can stop feeling like you're alone in the jungle and night is falling.

## Drums Say....

Getting on the grapevine routing list is easy. Get to know other designers in your area who have graphics computers. You can do this by contacting a dealer and asking who they've sold systems to, joining a users group, or asking a service bureau for the names of designers who bring in files for output.

You're going to need a good service bureau anyway, so find one and make them a part of your network. The people at the service bureau can be a tremendous resource, especially when making up a system list and evaluating software.

Ask the service bureau for the names of other studios that use graphics computers. Call these folks on the phone. Tell them you're about to purchase a graphics computer. Most will be very sympathetic. Over and over we hear that there's an infectious kind of enthusiasm that springs up in studios with graphics computers. Many are so excited they'll just burst if you don't let them tell you all about their system. If possible, visit a service bureau and a studio or two. Watch people working with the equipment. Ask questions. You'll quickly begin to form opinions about what works and what doesn't.

Even a casual browser can't help but be impressed with the number, variety, and heft of computer publications jamming the newsstands. It almost seems the publishers spew out enough computer literature to deforest several Amazon Basins each year.

The magazines—*MacWorld*, *MacUser*, *MacWeek*, *PC Week*, *Byte*, *Desktop,* et. al.—are a source of information for design studios. Not always a particularly *good* source of information, but a source nonetheless.

When the subject is automobiles, any uninformed reader can pick up a copy of *Car And Driver* and—an hour later—talk confidently about the thrilling turbo boost of the new Nissan 300ZX. Unfortunately, when it comes to computers, there are very few writers who have a solid background in graphic design, journalism, *and* the technical aspects of graphics production (such as the relationship of dot shape to four-color separation and printing). Until the advent of desktop publishing technology, many publishers kept their writers and production people in two separate worlds. Not enough time has gone by for the emergence of writers who are up to speed on the mechanics of graphic reproduction or of designers who can (or want to) write clearly about technology.

A welcome exception to this norm is *Step-By-Step Electronic Design*, a newsletter published by Dynamic Graphics that covers the nitty gritty of computer graphics techniques. *HOW Magazine*, published by F&W Publications, presents good case studies of studios that use graphics computers.

The general-circulation computer press, however, has a long way to go in covering graphic arts applications. When the publications test software and hardware for designers, they too often miss critical points of comparison.

One example is the confusion that once reigned in the desktop computer press over the relationship between dots per inch (which is how the resolution of laser printers and other image-setters is measured) and lines per inch (which is the traditional measure of the fineness of a halftone screen). The relationship is simple: There is none. The two measures are not directly comparable and aren't interchangeable when talking about the visual impression of a piece of printed material. A photograph scanned into a computer at 300 dots per inch and printed on a laser printer looks about as clear as an 85-line halftone printed on newsprint. When printed on an imagesetter at 1270 dots per inch, it improves to something approximating a 133-line halftone on glossy stock.

Fortunately, this situation is improving as production people trained on traditional equipment have gotten involved with the editorial staffs of the publications, helping evaluate products. Still, at the time of this writing, a current issue of a major magazine carried an article on scanners that casually averred that a typical black and white photograph was comprised of an "infinite" number of shades of gray. Certainly a good print should display a wide range of grays, but the number is nowhere near infinite. An average print may display fifteen distinct shades of gray. In his definitive book on black and white prints (*The Print*, Morgan & Morgan), Ansel Adams put the maximum *range* of tones for black and white prints (as measured by the amount of light they reflect) at 1:70 with a practical limit of 1:50. This distinction may seem minor, except that the author was using the allegedly "infinite" number of grays as a benchmark to measure the price-performance of gray-scale scanners.

Warts and all, computer publications are a necessary part of keeping in touch with the technology. For at least six months before and after you install a graphics computer, you should read one or more of the computer magazines. At the least, you'll get a steady diet of techno-talk that can help you better understand the ads, the sales-men, and the manuals.

### Reading Between The Lines

To get the information you need, you'll have to read between the lines. Don't assume that the writer knows more than you do, especially when it comes to design or mechanical reproduction. Very often what a review doesn't say is as revealing as what it does say. Don't assume that a filing program will solve your filing problems. If a facility or feature you think might be impor-tant (such as the ability of a filing program to print reports in a custom format that you specify) isn't mentioned in the review, there's every chance that it lacks the feature. However, reviewers can't possibly cover all the features of a program in the short space they're allotted. The reviewer may have felt the feature in ques-tion didn't warrant space in his report. As you read a review, make a mental list of the "miss-ing" features and ask someone who's used the program whether they exist. If you need a more immediate answer, call the software developer.

### Show Me The Way

The *way* in which a program works is just as important as *what* it does. As you read a soft-ware review, look carefully at the sections that talk about how the program works, rather than what it accomplishes. Think about whether you would be comfortable working in that way.

For example, two of the most popular page layout programs for the Macintosh are PageMaker® and Quark XPress®. PageMaker visually simulates a drafting board. It allows designers to "drag" objects off a page and into a margin area until they're needed, much as you'd put scraps of type on the edge of a drafting board. Many designers find that convenient, but

XPress did not have that facility until its most recent upgrade (3.0). However, the version of PageMaker current at the time of publication wouldn't allow you to have more than one document open at a time, while XPress lets you open up to seven documents simultaneously. The current version of XPress allowed placement of text at any angle, rotation of graphics within the program, and separation of continuous-tone color from within XPress itself without having to manually invoke external utilities. PageMaker didn't. Many designers say they find PageMaker easier to learn than XPress. Others say XPress gives them more powerful tools, especially for manipulating text, and that it works with a wider variety of graphics files. The nature of our work—producing highly illustrated art books and sophisticated print materials—demands the versatility of XPress. You'll have to decide which one suits your work and work habits best.

### Hard Choices

The same cautions apply to hardware reviews, though hardware reviews tend to be more accu-rate. Generally, reviewers have a good handle on the chips-and-wires aspects—they know what questions to ask, what benchmarks to use for measurement, and how to test for ease of use.

Getting the straight story on hardware at the leading edge of desktop computer applications —such as, at the moment, hardware for making separations from photographs—is much more difficult. You can't expect a reviewer at a gener-al computing magazine to know all the right questions and measurements to apply to equip-ment intended for color separation or three-dimensional drawing. You might expect the magazines to find specialists to evaluate special-ized gear, but they rarely do. If you intend to buy equipment for an advanced application, *you* need to know what the right questions are.

## Manufacturer's (Mis)Information

The stated purpose of advertising is not to inform but to persuade. That's its role in our economic scheme. Apply the same healthy skepticism you exercise when viewing auto advertising to ads for graphics computers.

Don't get us wrong—the number of vendors who purposely and consistently misrepresent their products is small. But there are some who insist on telling only the facts that are convenient. More prevalent and annoying than blatant fraud are vaporware and ignorance.

### A Case Of The Vapors

In the southern U.S., automobiles are sometimes struck by a malady known as "the vapors." The blistering heat of a mid-summer day can cause gasoline in the fuel line to boil, turning it from liquid to vapor. Since a car's fuel pump wasn't designed to pump vapor, it stops functioning. This leaves the driver stuck by the side of the road with a car that refuses to budge. Vaporware can do the same thing to your studio.

"Vaporware" is the computer industry's name for a product someone claims to be selling but can't be obtained or doesn't work.

For several years, Micropro, a large software developer, promised that a Macintosh version of WordStar®, its powerful word-processing package for IBM-compatibles, was "just around the corner." Mac WordStar was vaporware. Eventually, Micropro admitted Mac WordStar was nowhere near ready for market and that the company had dropped the project. WingZ®, a spreadsheet program, was "due for imminent release" for more than a year before it appeared.

The danger is that you may hear or read about a product that will make your studio run better or more productively. Its "imminent release" may convince you not to buy a competing product or not to take steps to address stumbling blocks in your computer operation because this product should solve them. Several large software developers have a reputation for trying to cripple their competitors' products by making spurious product announcements claiming to have a much better product that's almost ready for release. They're betting that a large number of buyers will hold off buying the competitor's product. If enough of them delay their purchase, the competitor might just drop the product, leaving the field clear for the "vaporware" developer to enter it.

If you're at the point of making a buying decision, there's an easy way to find out if a product is real: Call the manufacturer. The first question to ask is, "Are you shipping it?" If the answer is yes, ask for the name and telephone number of a dealer who has one, then call the dealer and ask if they have the item in stock. If not, it isn't real. Look for solutions elsewhere unless you can afford to wait.

### Fighting The "Duh Factor"

New computer vendors seem to pop up faster than mushrooms sprouting in cow pies after a spring rain. Not all of these new businesses are run by people who understand how printed materials are designed and produced. Too many press into their marketing campaigns before figuring out whether their hardware or software will be cost-effective—or even effective—in a design studio or print production shop.

Conversely, the engineers and programmers who create a terrific new product for designers may find themselves getting bored once the product is on the market. The turnover in Silicon Valley is staggering. If you have a highly technical question about how something works (or why it doesn't), and the product is several months old, there may not be anyone left at the vendor who understands it well enough to give you an answer.

We call this the "Duh Factor." That's the sound some support people make when you ask them highly technical questions about graphic arts applications, as in "Duhhhh, let me see if I can find someone who can help you."

The "Duh Factor" is one reason we tend to rely on major companies to meet our most important needs, rather than experimenting with solutions from small vendors. The major players —Aldus, Adobe, Xerox, Quark, Apple, MicroSoft, Borland *et. al.*—aren't likely to abandon a product line and generally provide good technical support. If you need an answer, you can get it. You may have to wait a day or two, but you can get it. There are many fine small vendors, and it's really not fair to tar them all with the same brush, but if there is a function in your studio that is critical to your business, the *safest* bet is to use a product from a large vendor.

The "Duh Factor" creeps into computer advertising, too. It's not uncommon for critical technical information to be left out. We recently requested information on a digital sound recorder for the Macintosh. The lavish brochure didn't list the recorder's frequency response or the number of synchronized channels that could be recorded simultaneously. We've seen ads for image scanners that didn't list the file formats supported by the software, and ads for drawing packages that didn't specify whether the program produced bit-mapped or vector graphics.

We look at computer advertising as a glorified product announcement: It's here; it may or may not be available, it may or may not work. *You* will have to determine what the most important criteria are for the products you buy. Again, your friends and service bureau are the most reliable sources of information.

## HYPE BUSTERS: Stop, Look, Listen, And Learn

It may be a jungle out there—a dark, scary, humid place with steaming heaps of promotional excess. But you can turn on the lights just by exercising a few basic precautions.

☐ Be very skeptical of new product reviews and product announcements.

☐ Early releases of hardware and software can be dicey, playing unexpected "tricks" on users. If you want to pioneer use of a new product, plan in the time to debug it.

☐ Compare reviews from several credible sources—different magazines, your friends, your service bureau.

☐ "Test drive" major purchases. Find a studio, dealer, or bureau who has the item and ask if you can use it for an hour.

☐ Know the criteria your purchases must meet. If output is destined for reproduction, find out whether or not the result is in fact reproducible. If you want to buy a film recorder for presentation slides, ask for samples and project them. Better yet, send a sample file to the manufacturer and ask that it be imaged on the film recorder.

☐ Don't over-research: If you wait for the perfect solution at the perfect price, you'll never buy. Don't waste time test driving things that cost $50, either. If the billable time needed to test something is worth more than the item costs, just buy it.

## To Market To Market: Where To Buy

Figuring out what to buy is hard enough, but once you know what you want, you still have to decide where to buy it: A local dealer? Mail order? And what about used equipment?

### Local Options

It's likely there's a dealer in your area who stocks, or can order, the system you want. While you may not be able to count on the dealer for reliable advice on what to buy, the ones we've dealt with were pretty good at helping us with the basic plug-this-into-that questions.

Whether or not you buy your equipment from a dealer, find a dealership with a good service technician. It's hard to evaluate a dealer's service department until you do, in fact, have something that needs service. Ask around; someone you know will have had experience with the local dealers. Knowing who to go to for quick, reliable service will minimize the disruption when a computer fails. Since most dealers can't give informed advice on buying graphics computers to designers, having a good service relationship is probably the strongest argument for buying equipment through a dealer. But the truth is that computers don't often fail. That makes it hard to justify paying a dealer's retail margins.

The more equipment you buy and the less you know about computers, the stronger the argument that you should use a local dealer. Most of them have experience troubleshooting network problems, hardware incompatibilities, and such. If you have a large installation, you're going to run into some of that. If the dealer sells you two pieces of equipment that won't talk to each other, he's obligated to make good on your order. If you buy two pieces that won't talk to each other, you're probably stuck. If you're confident you can install your system, consider buying direct from manufacturers or by mail order.

### Mail Order Savings

We've purchased all of our workstations through retail dealers, but bought the peripherals—hard disks, cabling, software, and scanners—through the mail. The workstations were purchased at retail because we found dealers who could come within a few percentage points of the mail order price. We felt it was worth an extra $100 per workstation to have someone local we could turn to if a problem developed. If the difference had been several hundred dollars, we wouldn't have bought from the dealer.

Our disk drives and peripherals were purchased through the mail because the local dealers couldn't match the prices. If you buy a bad hard disk from a manufacturer, you can return it for exchange just as you would with a dealer.

Dealers know what the mail order houses are charging. If you're buying an $11,000 system, you can bet there's a way for the dealer to squeeze his margin. You can help by being flexible on the brand of hard disk, for example; the dealer may have a lower cost on some brands.

### The Used Lot

Computers are generally very durable. A strong market has developed for used IBM-compatible machines and one is developing for used Macintosh computers. The things that wear out—the CRT and disk drive—can be replaced cheaply. Don't let a low price sucker you into buying yesterday's technology, however. Mac 512s and even the Mac Plus are probably not good investments for a design studio. Look for equipment that can be upgraded, such as the Macintosh SE/30 or Macintosh II. These are still close to the state of the art and can be upgraded easily. Have a service technician run a diagnostic on used gear before you buy, or get an iron-clad warranty from the dealer, especially mail-order dealers who charge your credit card.

# Chapter Six:
# Hardware Wars

*Hardware Wars: Apple Vs. IBM*

*The IBM Blues*

*PC To Mac—And Back*

*The Mac Attacked:*
*New Technologies On The Horizon*

*The Intangibles: It Just Feels Right*

Up to this point, we've been speaking as if all "graphics" computers are created equal. They aren't. For print graphics, there's the Macintosh and then there's everything else. If animation is important, you have to give a nod to the Commodore Amiga.

You'll notice there was no mention of IBM in the paragraph above. That's because few designers find IBM machines useful. Surveys indicate that Macs outnumber IBMs in design studios by more than three to one. Where IBMs have found a home in a graphics studio, they're used for business functions or—in a few instances—manipulation of color photographic images using the Truevision system of digitizer and display boards. For industrial designers or studios with a heavy orientation to packaging design, the IBM-compatible world has a great selection of CAD (Computer Aided Design) packages that can translate isometric drawings into three-dimensional objects. It's likely that the number of IBM-compatible machines in design studios will increase as designers begin to explore the capabilities of these three-dimensional programs and as more useful IBM graphics packages are developed. For now, however, there is no contest among designers; Macintosh wins hands down.

The reasons for this acceptance gap between the Macintosh and IBM-compatibles are both simple and complex. The simple reason is that the Macintosh has become the *de facto* standard in the graphic arts industry. There are more graphic arts software packages, more powerful illustration and layout software, more graphics peripherals, and more service bureaus supporting output from the Macintosh than any other desktop platform. If you want access to the "desktop computer power" you see talked about in the design press, at this point, you can only get it from a Macintosh. There are more powerful graphics computers available—such as the Quantel Paintbox®— but their prices can run into the *hundreds* of thousands instead of the tens of thousands. Systems, such as DuPont's Vaster® and Quantel, are very "narrow" platforms; software and peripherals for them are only available from their manufacturers. There are few third-party vendors (such as Adobe or Quark in the desktop world) to expand the capabilities of the machines or keep prices stable through competition.

The two most telling comments on this subject came from a service bureau and a publisher.

"If somebody asks me to print an occasional file from an IBM machine, I tell them to save it as a PostScript file and I'll run it," said Jim Davis, owner of Typesetting Today in Winter Park, Florida. "But if they want to set up a magazine or publication for us to run on a regular basis, I tell them to get a Macintosh."

Ziff-Davis Publishing Company, which owns *PC Computing Magazine, PC Magazine, PC Week, MacWeek,* and *MacUser,* is gradually moving all of its magazine production to desktop computers. The manager of computer operations, Lloyd Schultz, put it this way: "Anyone in production management would rather do pagination on a Macintosh than any other platform. *PC Magazine,* which doesn't allow Macintosh computers in its offices as a matter of principal, is trying to convert from manual production to doing production on an IBM-compatible system, and is paying for it dearly. In twenty months, they've only managed to get 20 percent of the magazine produced on the computer each month. *MacUser* and *MacWeek* are 100 percent produced on Macintosh."

At *MacWeek,* even the four-color photographs are scanned and separated on a Macintosh.

### Singing The Big Blue Blues

We know. Your clients all have IBMs. Maybe you do, too. The machines seem so much cheaper than a Macintosh—especially if you already have some. Before buying our first Macintosh, we had over $12,000 worth of IBM-compatible computer equipment in our studio. We still have most of it—stored in a closet. We keep thinking we'll find a use for it, but after three years, we're beginning to have our doubts. There are a number of design firms that use IBM-compatible computers for word processing, accounting, and billing—but not for serious graphics. Just put the notion of converting all those existing PCs to graphics workstations out of your mind. Every designer, every service bureau, every publisher we spoke with said the same thing: IBM-compatibles are terrific word processors. You can even do some page layout with them. They are not now and are not likely to become the tools of choice for professional artists.

The difference between the IBM PC and the Apple Macintosh is fundamental: The IBM PC was not conceived as a graphics computer. The Macintosh was. Everything about the Macintosh, from the way you interact with it to the language it uses to talk to printing devices, is geared to the creation of reproduction-quality artwork.

### The Techno-Babble

If you accept the premise of our last paragraph, you don't need to read this section. If you still hold out hope for IBM, or if you have a boss who doesn't believe in spending money for a Macintosh when there are extra PCs available in the office, read on.

All computers have a basic set of programming instructions called an *operating system*. The operating system defines the way in which the central processing unit (CPU) talks to its peripherals (disk drives, screen, printer), what kinds of manipulations of data it supports, how much memory it can use, and so on.

The operating system used on IBM compati-

bles is called MS-DOS (or PC-DOS). The initials stand for Microsoft Disk Operating System. The system was written by Microsoft, a large software developer, for IBM prior to the release of the original IBM PC. At the time, it was quite controversial. There was already a standard operating system for desktop computers called CPM (Control Program for Microcomputers) in widespread use. Industry observers speculated that having its own operating system would give IBM a marketing advantage if it could "lock out" other manufacturers, keeping them from making microcomputers that could exchange data with and use the same software as IBM PCs. With the threat of being incompatible with the world's largest computer maker in its arsenal, IBM's tremendous clout in the business market would ensure it the lion's share of microcomputer sales. In fact, this did work for a few years, until other manufacturers (Compaq, Epson, *et. al.*) found ways to make their machines think like the IBM PC and run MS-DOS software. In the meantime, CPM, a perfectly good operating system, and the millions of dollars worth of existing computers that used it were relegated to the junkyard. IBM and Microsoft racked up sales as business users flocked to this new "standard."

Score one for IBM. But MS-DOS is far from perfect. For one thing, the operating system has no provision for addressing more than 640 kb of RAM at one time. It's possible through a work-around scheme to have an MS-DOS machine with more than 640 kb of RAM (in fact, it's a necessity for running Ventura Publisher® or Aldus PageMaker®). But DOS computers can't have more than 640 kb of program code resident in primary memory at any given time.

This is a severe handicap in the world of graphics. Compared to sales figures or name-and-address type data, graphics require an enormous amount of memory. A thousand words take up about 7 kb of memory, while a single grayscale scan of a photograph takes up 300 kb. Manipulating photographs or color illustrations—rotating, resizing, making color separations—requires 2–4 mb of RAM or more.

The software programs needed to perform these manipulations are themselves massive: The main file alone of Quark XPress® (never mind the dictionary for the spell-checker or the style-tag files) is 840 kb; Illustrator®, Freehand®, and Digital Darkroom® are each about 450 kb. While not all of a program's code needs to be held in RAM at one time, the more code that's in RAM, the faster the program will run. If part of the code is not in RAM, the computer may have to repeatedly read new sections of the program from its disk drive. The CPU is forced to ask for the code, then wait while the disk drive finds, retrieves, and passes it on. As of this writing, the Macintosh logic board would hold—and the operating system could directly address—up to 8 mb of RAM. Upgrades planned for 1990–1991 would allow it to hold and address up to 32 mb of RAM. Additionally, with a $300 upgrade, Macintosh users can use their hard disks as RAM. Even if you have only 1 mb of physical RAM located inside your computer, up to 14 mb of blank hard disk space can be used as if it were RAM.

Another problem with the IBM design is that the PC, XT, and AT machines are "eight-bit" computers. The electrical "highways" along which data moves between and through the components are "eight lanes" wide; eight bits of data (or one byte) can pass at one time. The Macintosh, however, is a thirty-two bit computer. Its "highways" allow thirty-two bits of data (four bytes) to move simultaneously. A thirty-two lane highway can accommodate a lot more cars than an eight-lane road. Cars can travel faster, too.

These comparative shortcomings of DOS were pointed out by Apple Computer's advertis-

ing. They have been underscored by the graphic arts marketplace, in which IBM-compatible machines are scarce. IBM and Microsoft set out to even the score. First, they wrote extensions to DOS to allow it to address more than 640 kb of RAM. Unfortunately, DOS still considers this extended RAM as a second-class citizen and can't use it as effectively as the first 640 kb.

Microsoft then created a new operating system, called OS/2 (Operating System 2). Amid a promotional blitzkrieg predicting doom for the Macintosh, OS/2 was released in 1988. It was greeted with fervent yawns by the computer industry.

OS/2 did address some of the fundamental design limitations of MS-DOS. OS/2 operates on IBM-compatible sixteen-bit machines and supports multi-tasking—the ability to have several different software programs open and active at the same time. However, compared to the Macintosh, it was seen as too little, too late. Software developers have stayed away in droves. Early in 1990, Microsoft showed an experimental version of OS/2 2.0. It supported thirty-two bit data paths and offered some interesting memory enhancements. However, industry observers predicted the full release of OS/2 2.0 was "many months" away. Writing graphics software to take advantage of its features would take even longer.

This brings us to a critical comparison between IBM-compatibles and Macintosh: The software programs themselves. Without software programs to express and carry out your commands, a computer is slightly less useful than a broken toaster. Speed and graphics-crunching power are strikes one and two against IBM DOS machines; graphics software is an emphatic strike three.

There are MS-DOS graphics programs that are useful to designers: CrystalPaint®, Lumena®, and the programs that run on the AT&T/Truevision TARGA boards for example. There's even a

DOS version of Adobe Illustrator, but there is no equivalent of the Macintosh version of Illustrator or FreeHand—the two "backbone" drawing programs for Macintosh. Micrografx Designer® and Corel Draw® have been touted as contenders to the Macintosh drawing programs. In fact, the results achieved in Micrografx Designer are quite good (see pages 26–27).

Despite the recent appearance of quality graphics software for DOS computers, designers need a seamless web of software that allows them to create professional-quality illustrations, scan in photos, manipulate them, then combine the photos with type and output them at a quality suitable for lithographic reproduction. At the time of publication, it was *possible* to do that with an IBM-compatible system using Designer or Illustrator and PageMaker, but the range of effects available to the designer were limited. For Macintosh, that web of software is strong. The number of competing programs that fit into it—and the number of creative manipulations that can be performed on illustrations, type, and photos—is large and growing rapidly.

The OS/2 operating system may, in time, allow IBM-compatible machines to do most of the things the Macintosh has been doing since 1988. At the moment, however, there is no full-featured set of graphics packages for illustration, design, and layout that will even run under OS/2 (let alone run well enough to challenge the abilities of a Macintosh). Also, the OS/2 system software sucks up a lot of the computer's power, reserving too much for itself and making too little available for the applications software.

If you still think OS/2 is your ticket, consider this: You probably won't be able to use the PCs you already have to run OS/2.

By adopting OS/2, IBM split its machines into two classes. The older IBM PCs and XTs with 8086 CPU chips won't run OS/2 without a major (and expensive) hardware upgrade to the newer 80386 or 80486 CPU chip. It's possible to run OS/2 on IBM AT-class computers with 80286 CPUs, but the demands of OS/2 would probably choke the 80286 CPU, slowing graphic transformations and screen redraw to a crawl.

Replacing the motherboard of an older PC with an 80386 motherboard roughly equivalent in basic computing power to that of a Macintosh II (a 25-mhz 80386 with cache memory and 2 mb of RAM) cost $4,100 in early 1990. A brand-new 80386-based computer with a two-page monitor and enough RAM to run OS/2 cost about $5,000. At the same time, a complete Macintosh IIx with 2 mb of RAM and a two-page monitor also had a list price of about $5,000. Cheaper upgrades for IBM-compatible computers were available, but they did 't include extra RAM or memory caches and ran at speeds only marginally faster than the original IBM PC—far too slow for serious graphics work.

While machines that run OS/2 will also run MS-DOS applications, the two aren't interchangeable. MS-DOS graphics software doesn't run significantly faster on computers with 80386 CPUs than it does on an 80286 computer.

That puts designers who would like to use IBM-compatible machines for graphic arts into a neat Catch 22: If you're hoping that MS-DOS graphics software (which will run on your existing IBM PC compatible) will someday catch up to the level of Macintosh software, don't hold your breath. MS-DOS doesn't have the power and DOS developers are a good two years behind Macintosh developers in graphics software. OS/2 is IBM's admission that its MS-DOS based machines won't perform as well as a Macintosh for graphics applications. If, on the other hand, you decide to use an OS/2 system, you'll have to either buy an IBM-compatible with an 80386 or 80486 CPU or pay for an expensive upgrade to your existing equipment. Then, you'll have to wait and hope that developers take a shine to OS/2 and invest huge sums in the development of graphics software for it—software that already exists for the Macintosh.

That seems like quite a gamble to us. In the two years since the release of OS/2, not one major OS/2 graphics package has been released. During that same time, the Macintosh community has seen the introduction of Adobe Illustrator, Aldus FreeHand, PixelPaint®, Adobe Photo-Shop®, PhotoMac®, Digital Darkroom®, Letra-Studio®, Canvas 2®, MacroMind Director®, and dozens of other graphics programs.

Assuming that IBM doesn't abandon OS/2 and release yet another operating system, OS/2 software development is likely to take several years. It seems assured that, by the time effective graphics applications are available for OS/2, developers will have added dozens more graphics programs to the Macintosh repertoire.

### It's A Mac World After All

If you choose not to use a Macintosh, you will be opting out of the largest installed user base of graphics computers. What's an installed user base? That's techno-talk for the number of people who have a particular computer or software program. It's what developers count when they decide whether to make their whiz-bang new software program run on an IBM or an Apple. The developers have already spoken: The preponderance of high-end graphics packages being released run on Macintosh, not IBM. The graphic arts industry has spoken: The preponderance of desktop computers used by graphic arts service firms (typesetters, service bureaus, prepress shops) are Macintosh. The design studios have spoken: The vast majority of graphics computers in use in design studios are Macintosh. By the time TARGA graphics catch on among designers, many of them will already have made heavy investments in Macintosh. They're more

likely to add an IBM-compatible or two to their pool of Macintosh workstations than they will be to "go over" to an IBM standard.

When it comes to finicky gizmos like computers, there's a lot to be said for knowing other people who have the same equipment you do. If you opt to install IBM-compatible workstations, you'll be placing yourself outside of the vast, easy-to-access Macintosh support network that exists in the graphic arts industry.

### PC To Mac—And Back

The next question, of course, is how a Macintosh-based design studio can exchange text files and other data with clients—or with its own administrative workers—who rely on IBM compatibles. Very easily is how. There are several solid, proven ways to do this.

When IBM released DOS, it did so in part to prevent the exchange of software and data between its computers and those made by other manufacturers. IBM has consistently ignored the trend in the computer business toward "connectivity," the ability of computers made by different manufacturers, running different operating systems, to talk to each other and cooperate.

While IBM had its head in the sand on connectivity, other manufacturers, including Apple, were working to implement it. There are at least three ways to transfer data between IBM PCs and the Macintosh: networks, modems, and direct disk transfer.

A network is simply a group of computers tied together by a communications link. All Macintosh computers are built with the ability to participate in a network. IBM PCs and compatibles require extra hardware to be put on a network. The developers who created the software (such as TOPS®) and hardware for these communications links have made it possible to mix IBM-compatibles and Macintosh computers on one network. The data being sent through the network can be received and used by any computer on the network as long as the data is structured in a way that is understood by both machines. Fortunately, there are standards for this. Text created in an MS-DOS word processing program (such as WordStar®, WordPerfect®, or MS-Word®) can be saved as an ASCII text file. That file can then be transferred through the network to a Macintosh and imported into Page-Maker, XPress, or some other page layout program. Financial data from spreadsheets can be saved in the SYLK format and transferred from Lotus 1-2-3® (a ubiquitous MS-DOS spreadsheet program) to Excel®, WingZ®, Trapeze®, or some other spreadsheet on the Macintosh.

A utility provided by Apple, called Apple File Exchange, performs direct translation for converting Lotus 1-2-3 files to Excel format and MS-Word files to Macintosh format without saving them as a SYLK or ASCII file. Apple File Exchange translators for other MS-DOS programs are also available. To use the utility, you find the MS-DOS file you want to translate on the network, open it with File Exchange, then save it as a Macintosh file.

While "network" can mean a group of computers in widely scattered locations, in the context of desktop computers, it usually means a group of computers in the same office. To take files from a client whose computers are not connected with yours, you can use a modem link or disk transfer.

You simply have your client send you ASCII or SYLK files over the telephone via modem. Your Macintosh will receive and record the files, which can then be opened and placed in a word processor, page layout program, or spreadsheet. There are communications services, such as GEnie, CompuServe, and MCI Mail, which maintain "mailboxes" for computer users. By renting a mailbox, you can have clients send text and other documents to your mailbox, then retrieve them at your leisure. This makes modem transfers almost painless, since the communication services' computers are set up to make transfers as foolproof as possible.

It's even possible to send color layouts and other graphics back and forth. A studio in San Francisco said it recently demonstrated this to a client in Australia, sending color graphics via telephone for viewing on the client's computers.

Another proven method for moving text and data from PC to Mac is just to transfer it by floppy disk. The Macintosh "super" floppy disk drive, which has been standard issue on all Macintosh II models made since 1988, can read disks created by IBM-compatibles. The only catch is that the IBM has to have a 3 $\frac{1}{2}$-inch, 1.44 mb floppy drive (common on later XT- and AT-class machines). Apple File Exchange can then be used to translate the data from the disk.

Several manufacturers make disk drives for the Macintosh that will read the 5 $\frac{1}{4}$-inch diskettes used with IBM-compatibles that lack a 3 $\frac{1}{2}$-inch drive. You just plug the drive into the back of your Macintosh, slip in an IBM-format disk, and away you go.

If none of these solutions sound feasible, try this: You can turn your Macintosh into an MS-DOS computer. SoftPC® is a software package that fully emulates an 80286 computer, allowing your Macintosh to open and even run MS-DOS programs, such as Lotus 1-2-3, WordStar and Ashton-Tate's Dbase®. Or, you can add a circuit board to your Macintosh that contains a full-bore 80386 computer. Again, it makes your Mac work just like an IBM-compatible, and you can cut-and-paste information between the DOS programs and the Macintosh to your heart's content.

Another easy way of converting files from MS-DOS to Macintosh format is to take them to your service bureau. Most service bureaus will do this cheaply or even free.

The reasons for buying a Macintosh can be summarized as more power, more users, more immediate applications. IBM's position can be summarized simply: When will they catch up? There is a place for IBM graphics applications. But for now, that place is decidedly not as the *primary* tools of a professional design studio. Some designers and publishers say they get along quite well with an IBM system. If you want to use a graphics computer to set type, you can do that with an IBM or compatible. If, however, you want access to the broadest range of graphics software, at this time Macintosh is the way. Not even the powerful Sun workstations have the variety of illustration, color separation, and layout packages offered for the Macintosh. Studios which use IBM computers for graphics tend to have a much larger number of Macintosh workstations networked with one or two IBMs.

From a price-performance perspective, Macintosh is also clearly the winner for design studios. This is ironic, since most people think of Macintosh as more expensive than MS-DOS machines. What the manufacturers aren't telling you is that full-featured graphics applications for IBM-compatible machines won't run on the inexpensive clones. To run the best IBM compatible graphics software, you'll need a computer that costs just as much as a Macintosh.

## A Level Playing Field?

The cost of a complete graphics computer system is not small. You have to think about how long you have to recover its cost; how long before more investment will be needed; how long before the technology you purchased is superseded by better, more cost-effective products; whether your system is going to be a dead end or whether you can upgrade it as new technologies appear.

From a financial point of view, think of a graphics computer as a three-year investment. Whatever you buy today will not be the "state of the art" for more than three years. Of course, a three-year-old computer will still operate. It can continue performing the tasks that justified its purchase in the first place. But by then, you'll probably be ready to upgrade by buying a newer machine or adding to the existing one. You will likely want hardware and software that do more. From that perspective, installing a graphics computer is a continuing investment. As you find more products that enhance your studio's performance, you'll want to buy them.

Looking into the future is risky, but it doesn't appear that the Macintosh will become a dead end or a dinosaur in 1991, 1992, or 1993. Its primacy in the graphic arts will be challenged by other computer manufacturers including IBM, Sun, NeXT, and others. It's unlikely—but not impossible— that one of these could become the new standard in the graphic arts by 1994. It's much more likely that the most useful Macintosh software will be adapted or replicated for use on other computers. There are two technologies that could hasten the advent of a "level playing field," where the Macintosh or its successors would have to share the graphic arts market with other systems. As you plan your investment in graphic arts computers, keep in mind that these technologies could change the market conditions, creating more competition for Macintosh (and holding down its price while spurring improvements in performance) or creating a lot of confusion (freezing developers in their tracks as they try to sort out which platform they should be writing software for).

***RISC:*** In early 1990, IBM released a dramatically revamped version of its Reduced Instruction Set Computers (RISC), the System/6000. Sun, with its SPARCstations, was already a major player in this technology (which was invented by IBM).

In a traditional microcomputer, one CPU does most of the thinking. It therefore must be very versatile, and the list of instructions it needs to perform all of its tasks is long. When it's asked to do one of the tasks on the list by a software program, the CPU has to read through the list to find the instruction before it can load and execute it. This takes time. Meanwhile, all other computer operations, such as reading data from disk or writing to the screen, are put on hold.

RISC processors, on the other hand, employ several CPUs working together. Each one is specialized and contains a much shorter list of commands; a reduced set of instructions. Because the list of commands is shorter, the CPU spends less time looking for instructions and more time executing them, speeding things up considerably. RISC-type computers with specialized graphics circuit boards could bring the full power of today's professional pre-press workstations onto your desktop. It's interesting to note that, while continuous tone color separations are being done on Macintosh machines, there are several proprietary color-separation systems (such as the CyberChrome unit) that are built around IBM-compatible rather than Macintosh hardware.

If another manufacturer can knock Macintosh off its perch, it will probably be with a RISC workstation. Apple may try to prevent this by implementing some form of RISC in the Macintosh line or introducing its own RISC computers.

Apple has partially responded to this challenge already. Early in 1990, it released the Macintosh IIfx. The real bottleneck in most microcomputers is the time needed for the CPU to talk to the peripherals—the screen, an external hard disk, or the floppy disk. Apple assigned the drudgery of communicating with the disk drives and other peripherals to two subordinate CPUs, the same chip used as the main processor in an Apple IIe. In addition, the IIfx has a main CPU that is blisteringly fast by 1990 standards: It runs at 40 mhz, three times as fast as the CPU in the average IBM PC-AT and half again as fast as the CPU in the entry-level IBM System/6000 machines.

In 1990, RISC machines weren't yet price-competitive: The lowest-priced RISC station available cost $13,000 (which included a 120 mb hard disk, 8 mb of RAM, and a nineteen-inch monochrome monitor). A similarly equipped Macintosh could be had for less than $8,000. The price of the Macintosh IIfx was not set at press time, but was projected to be approximately $12,000.

*UNIX:* This is an operating system that offers very powerful tools for the manipulation of graphic images. It's widely used by scientists and governmental agencies. Versions of Unix are available for computers made by a number of different manufacturers, including AT&T, IBM, Sun, Apple Macintosh, Digital Equipment Company, and others. At the moment, however, the graphics software available for the Macintosh does not run under Unix.

The promise of Unix is that, were it to become *the* standard operating system for desktop computers, software could be developed that could be "ported" easily. "Porting" is the word for modifying program code so that it will run on a different brand of hardware. The discrepancy between the capabilities of software running on an Apple and software running on an IBM would be reduced.

The IBM and Sun RISC workstations run proprietary versions of Unix. Apple has had a version of Unix for the Macintosh, called A/UX, for several years. Early in 1990 it demonstrated an enhanced version of A/UX that let the user run Unix applications and Macintosh applications simultaneously. The new A/UX had the familiar look and feel of standard Macintosh software. If Unix becomes the operating system of choice in the graphic arts, Macintosh users should be able to make the transition without having to undergo the shock of learning a batch of new commands.

Everyone worries about paying $12,000 to $20,000 for a piece of equipment that will be obsolete before it's paid for. That's not likely to happen to either the upper-end IBM-compatible or Macintosh computers. In both cases, the framework on which to expand capabilities is there. However, at this time, the clear lead in realizing those capabilities for designers belongs to Macintosh.

## The Intangibles: It Just Feels Right

There is one more area of comparison between brands of computers. That's the intangible but all-important "hands on factor." What does it feel like to spend the better part of your workday parked in front of this machine? There is a contagious enthusiasm that seems to accompany the arrival of a Macintosh in a design studio. For some reason, whether because of the clunky feeling of the operating system or the paucity of really gee-whiz software, IBM-compatible computers don't seem to spark the same kind of creative fire ignited by the Macintosh. We've never met a designer who was emotionally *passionate* about an MS-DOS computer. Those who use MS-DOS computers say things like, "It works pretty well." Macintosh users buttonhole acquaintances and frantically preach to them about Macintosh, generally acting like Hare Krishnas selling *Godhead* at O'Hare Airport on a holiday weekend.

There is a reason for this. It goes back to the creators of the machines.

### PARCing Permit

IBM machines were conceived by and for left-brained people who appreciate order and whose main concern is to describe the world by means of numbers. Their world is one of linear processes. And in that world, MS-DOS computers are wonderful tools: they're nimble, quick, and able to describe, simulate, and project reality with a high degree of accuracy.

The Macintosh is the most commercially successful product of the efforts of a long line of right-brained, non-linear thinkers who felt computers were too important to be entrusted solely to people who understand differential calculus.

When it was introduced, there were two features that distinguished the Macintosh from other desktop computers: one technical, one philosophical. The first was the use of Adobe's PostScript page description language. This freed the Macintosh from the fetters of replicating graphics by reducing them to checkerboard-like bit maps. Instead, PostScript allowed the Mac to describe the world in terms of vectors. This meant that the Macintosh could be hooked up to a wide range of printing devices and that the quality of the output would be determined by the quality of the printer rather than by the Macintosh software. This lead to the first true reproduction-quality type and illustration available on a desktop computer.

The second was the use of a GUI (graphical user interface).

GUI is a legacy of research done at the Palo Alto Research Center (PARC) for Xerox in the late 1970s. To make the power of computers accessible to the widest variety of people, a small band of programmers felt that the old way of communicating with a computer—by typing arcane commands like "LOAD.BAT" on a keyboard—had to change. They developed an operating system that used pictures to represent files, software programs, or actions. The user could point to the desired action with a hand-held pointing device (called a mouse) and by clicking a button, instruct the computer to load and run the file.

Much of the "catch up" work done by IBM and Microsoft over the past four years has been to create a GUI that's as easy to use and as effective as that of the Macintosh. Although they have come up with two alternatives, Windows (which runs under MS-DOS) and Presentation Manager (which runs under OS/2), no one has even vaguely suggested them as true competitors to the Macintosh.

The result of this rift between DOS and Macintosh, between the keyboard and GUI, is that the Macintosh thinks like you do: non-linear, visual, result-oriented rather than sequence-oriented. We believe it's the recognition of a kindred spirit (embodied in the programming code of the GUI) that designers respond to.

With a whole lot of effort—and at a considerable cost—DOS machines can be made to act something like a Macintosh. The question is: Why bother?

90

# Chapter Seven:
# Building A Shopping List

**A Computer On Every Desk?**

**Which Jobs Should You Automate First?**

**Shopping For Systems: Forewarned Is Forearmed**

**CPUs And The Need For Speed**

**All In The Family: A Plenitude Of Peripherals**

**Printers, Scanners, And RAM**

**Software Selector**

**Pulling Together The Pieces**

**Penny-Pinching Production**

## A Computer On Every Desk?

If you're only buying one graphics computer, your decisions are easy. Figure out what you need and write the check. If you're buying a system for a multi-designer studio, however, it's a bit more complicated. How many systems should you buy, and of what type? Since the late 1960s, futurists have been echoing Franklin Roosevelt's Depression-era pledge of a "chicken in every pot and a car in every garage," promising us a hard disk on every desk and a computer on every credenza. For design studios, that time will undoubtedly come. But not in 1990. There has to be an economic justification for having a computer on every desk.

Generally, design studios have been conservative in their purchases. In the majority of studios we contacted, there is not yet a computer on every desk. The ratio of machines to designers seems to hover between four people to three machines and seven people to five machines. There are extremes at both ends, and because the technology is so new, to quote any number as an average that is effective or normal would be misleading. In our studio and others, there's a workstation at every desk. Other firms have "pooled" their computers, creating a computer bullpen, with the keyboard crowd feeding type, illustrations, and completed page layouts back to senior designers who work at art tables.

### Start At The Bottom Of The Stack?

You can't just lay computer hardware on every desk and expect the troops to jump up and cheer. Not everyone *wants* a computer on their desk. In studios with more than seven designers, there are enough different personalities that you can expect resistance to this change. You may find it in a studio of only three designers, too. Studio managers say resistance to adopting computers is most frequent among designers with a few years of traditional design experience. They may feel that their methods get the job done and changing tools at this point in their development will literally cramp their style, causing them to redefine work habits acquired over many years and many projects.

There's another side to this, though: Some studio managers said they've interviewed younger designers who were very reluctant to work in a studio that didn't offer them a computer of their own. Experienced designers who've converted to full-time computer-aided design have also echoed those sentiments. So, while graphics computers may alienate some designers, there are also talented designers who won't consider working with you unless you work with computers.

When considering how many computers to buy and how fast to bring them in, think carefully about yourself and your associates. There's no sense in making payments on a piece of gear that's sitting idle. Having too few machines can cause trouble, too. In studios where most of the designers are computer users and where designers outnumber computers by more than two to one, there's competition for computer time. You may find yourself playing referee, pushing some designers' work off to get another project through faster. No matter how logical or fair you are, that's going to create problems.

If your designers are clamoring for graphics computers, your problem will be rationing the workstations you can afford. *If your designers aren't clamoring for computers, take time out for an orientation.* Almost everyone knows what graphics computers are. But seeing them actually *work* can be enlightening. Visit a service bureau or another studio *en masse*. This gives everyone a chance to see what all the fuss is about, to ask questions of people who are knowledgeable about the equipment and the process, and to be reassured that this isn't a plot to make their lives difficult.

*When you feel everyone is somewhat informed, talk to them as a group about the advantages and disadvantages.* Somehow the frustrations of learning to use a complex drawing program become more manageable when you spell out the relationship between graphics computers, designer productivity, net profit, and their paycheck. It wouldn't be wise to make predictions about the size of increased profits until you have some experience with the equipment because they won't materialize overnight and they depend on a lot of external variables (clients, for example). Soliciting the input of your associates, however, will give everyone an equal opportunity to understand why and how the change will come about, what their roles can be, and what the benefits are down the road.

A strategy that's worked for some studios is to add computers at "the bottom of the stack." Give the first computers to the people who do the most production. Production artists are usually ecstatic about anything that makes their job easier. Also, the payback from your investment can be realized most quickly through lower production costs. The computers can be given to people who will accept them, your investment will begin paying dividends immediately, and you won't appear to be forcing a senior designer to throw out his airbrush. As the production people increase their skills, designers will see that the computer is a valuable tool and start working with it. Buy one extra workstation; it can serve as a back-up and as an open workstation, inviting everyone to begin experimenting.

---

### TASK FORCE: Decide Which Functions You'll Automate First

A gradual transition is likely to be smoothest. Lessons learned at one stage will help with subsequent buying decisions. Check the boxes next to the functions you want to transfer in the first stage of your transition. See the charts on pages 96 and 103 for equipment choices.

#### Stage One

☐ Type design/selection  ☐ Repro type
☐ Rough layouts  ☐ Mechanical art
☐ Client comps

#### Stage Two

☐ Conceptual design  ☐ Slides/business presentations
☐ Positioning images  ☐ Logotypes/Font creation
☐ Illustrations  ☐ Telecommunication
☐ Film negatives  ☐ Job estimating
☐ Spot color separations  ☐ Scheduling/tracking

#### Stage Three

☐ Photo imaging and separation  ☐ Animation
☐ Full color computer design  ☐ Three-dimensional design
☐ Video  ☐ Billing/accounting

## Shopping For Systems: Forewarned Is Forearmed

By now, you should have a good handle on what you want your graphics computer to do. Using the task list from the preceding page, you can build an equipment list. This shopping list is your way of warding off unwelcome peddlers who will press unnecessary hardware on you. Remember your plan and stick to essentials, especially when buying your first computer. You can add accessories after you have the basic system in place. Don't under-buy either. If you're going to do a lot of illustration, buy a scanner; if you plan to do a large volume of mechanical production, buy a large monitor.

The hardware chart (overleaf) and software chart (page 103) are broken down by task, and the tasks are again divided into three stages.

### Going Slow Versus Going All The Way

Unless you already have some experience with graphics computers and have a strong client-driven demand for color graphics (for packaging or animation, for example), we recommend not buying equipment for the third stage until you've worked with a graphics computer for at least six months. Otherwise, you'll be making payments on expensive equipment that—for the short term—you won't be able to fully use. Whether you should buy the gear listed in stages one and two all at once depends on your affinity for computers and how fast you want to get maximum productivity from them.

If you like machines, if you've operated computer-driven typesetting equipment or other pre-press gear, if you want to move into computer illustration as quickly as possible, if you need to produce complex mechanicals, or if you plan to produce a large volume of mechanicals, you're a good candidate to buy for stage one and stage two immediately.

The best way to learn how to use a graphics computer is to use it; it's hard to absorb the actual techniques from a book. Going directly to stage two will likely shorten the amount of time it takes to fully integrate the computers into your work—you'll have the hardware and software available, you'll use it, and your skills will increase quickly. On the short term, this could be somewhat confusing, simply because you'll have more pieces of equipment and more software packages to deal with immediately.

For some reason, small studios seem to move from stage one to stage two more quickly than large studios. It seems to take longer for computer skills to diffuse through a larger organization.

### Choosing The CPU

The first two columns on the hardware chart (overleaf)—basic CPU and advanced CPU—represent a critical decision: whether to buy a lower-performance, lower-priced Macintosh Plus or Macintosh SE, or whether you should buy a Macintosh SE/30 or one of the various Macintosh II models.

We wouldn't recommend an IBM or IBM-compatible as the first graphics computer in any design studio (see *Penny-Pinching Production*, page 106 and *Hardware Wars*, page 81). You may want to add IBM-compatibles in the second or third stage of your transition as your use of business and three-dimensional software increases.

As in most things, you get what you pay for. If you don't intend to move beyond stage one, a Macintosh Plus or SE will be very cost-effective. They will let you do basic page makeup and some light-duty illustration work at the minimum cost. However, don't expect them to grow with your needs and skills. They don't support color monitors and software or provide much in the way of upgrade capability, although the SE does have one expansion slot for a large monitor display board or other accessories. Upgrade capability is especially important if you plan to do color, animation, three-dimensional design, or photographic separations at some point.

If you feel you'll "top out" at stage two for a year or two, a Macintosh SE or SE/30 can work well for you. However, if you plan to work into the advanced functions in stage two or get into stage three at any time in the next two years, start with an SE/30 or a Macintosh II. Apple seems to have settled on the Macintosh II as its basic platform for the foreseeable future. As new models have been introduced (IIx, IIcx, IIci, and IIfx), upgrades have been offered to bring older models up to the latest specifications.

## All About Chips

The "box"—the CPU unit that houses the CPU chip, circuit boards, and internal disk drives—is the heart of any graphics computer system. Since CPUs can cost almost as much as an automobile, you owe it to yourself to at least learn the points of comparison between them.

The place to start is with the CPU chip itself and the data paths that carry information to and from the CPU.

While still functional and useful, the older Macintosh Plus and SE designs are showing their age. These machines were built around the Motorola 68000 CPU chip. Although the machines have thirty-two bit data paths, the 68000 is a sixteen-bit chip. It's considerably slower than the newer 68020 chips (used in the Macintosh II) or the the 68030 (SE/30, IIx, IIcx, IIci, and the new IIfx). A new release of the Apple System file (version 7.0) is planned for mid-1990. How well it will run on the older 68000 CPU is unknown. While various accelerators (see page 98) and upgrades are available to make 68000-based machines run faster, you wouldn't want to buy a Plus or an SE as the base unit for a full-bore graphics computer system.

The early Macintosh models, including the Plus, had a fatal flaw: Apple didn't put sockets on their logic boards to accept additional circuit boards. Having these sockets, called "expansion slots," means the computer's performance can be increased or its capabilities expanded by installing new circuit cards later. The original IBM PC, released back in 1978, had expansion slots. That fact contributed mightily to their longevity; many of these original PCs are still in service a decade later, having been expanded over the years. To be fair, some of the first Macintosh units (128k and 512k E models) are also still in service; more than a few of them in design studios. But without an easy way to upgrade, these models have become evolutionary dead ends, for the most part.

It's not entirely clear why it took Apple so long to get with the program. Apple released three models of the Macintosh before it added a solitary expansion slot to the Macintosh SE.

The Macintosh II, released in 1987, was Apple's first fully expandable Macintosh, with six expansion slots—called "NuBus slots"—on the logic board. It was also the first modular Macintosh. The CPU, monitor, and disk drives of the Plus and SE are integrated in a single cabinet. The Mac II is a flat, rectangular case with a separate monitor.

When evaluating Macintosh CPUs and CPU chips, it's important to keep track of the speed offered by the various CPU chips. The "clock speed" of a CPU is measured in megahertz (mhz); 1 mhz equals one thousand cycles per second. The number of cycles tells you how many times per second the CPU "resets" itself, carrying out the next step of an instruction, looking for new instructions to carry out, or sending data to the screen, disk drive, or other chips for further processing. Not all instructions can be completed in one cycle. If the average instruction requires seven cycles to complete, and the

## CPUs And The Need For Speed

### HARD CHOICES: Creating A System List That Serves Your Needs

This chart is just a guide. You're the only one who knows what you want to accomplish, how much new equipment your studio is capable of absorbing, and how heavily you will rely on the computers. For each of the tasks, we've keyed the chart to show what equipment you must have, pieces that are strongly recommended, and pieces that are optional. In each case the "must have" pieces are those that are essential; you can't get the job done effectively without them. The "strongly recommended" items will increase productivity or enhance your capability in that area. "Optional" equipment is extremely useful, but not critical.

Key: M: Must have  S: Strongly recommend  O: Optional

| | Basic CPU | Advanced CPU | Accelerator | Large Monitor | 40 mb Disk | 60-100 mb disk | PostScript Printer | Image Scanner | Extra RAM | Drawing Tablet | Network Hdwre | Color Monitor | Color Printer | Film Recorder |
|---|---|---|---|---|---|---|---|---|---|---|---|---|---|---|
| **Stage One** | | | | | | | | | | | | | | |
| Type design/selection | M | | | | M | O | M | | | | | | | |
| Rough layouts | M | | S | | M | O | S | | | | | | | |
| Comps | M | | S | | M | O | M | S | | | | | | |
| Repro type | M | | | | M | O | S | | | | | | | |
| Mechanical art | M | | S | | M | O | M | | | | | | | |
| **Stage Two** | | | | | | | | | | | | | | |
| Conceptual design | M | S | | M | M | S | M | S | | O | | O | O | |
| Positioning images | M | | S | | | M | S | M | S | | | | | |
| Illustrations | M | S | O | S | | M | M | S | S | O | | O | O | |
| Film negatives | M | | | | | M | | | | | | | | |
| Spot color separations | M | S | | | | M | S | S | O | | | S | O | |
| Slides | M | S | | O | | M | M | O | O | | | M | S | O |
| Logotypes | M | | | O | M | | M | O | | | | O | O | |
| Telecommunications | M | | | | M | | | | | | | | | |
| Estimating | M | | | | M | | | | | | | | | |
| Scheduling/tracking | M | | | | M | | | | | | | | | |
| **Stage Three** | | | | | | | | | | | | | | |
| Photo imaging/separation | M | O | S | | | M | M | M | M | | | M | S | |
| Full color computer design | M | O | S | M | | M | S | M | M | | | M | M | O |
| Video | M | O | S | M | | M | S | M | M | | | M | S | O |
| Animation | M | S | S | M | | M | S | M | M | O | | M | S | O |
| Three-dimensional design | M | S | S | M | | M | S | M | M | O | | S | | O |
| Billing/accounting | M | | | | | | M | | | | | | | |

CPU runs at 7 mhz, then the CPU can process one million instructions per second, or one MIP.

The relationship between the clock speed of the CPU and how fast you can rotate a logo on the screen is not one-to-one. A 20 mhz CPU won't spin it twice as fast as a 10 mhz CPU, but clock speed *does* matter—and faster is definitely better. The 68020 used in the Macintosh II has a clock speed of 16 mhz. The Macintosh SE/30, IIx, IIcx, and IIci use 68030 CPU chips with clock speeds of 16 to 25 mhz. The Macintosh IIfx runs at 40 mhz. IBM PCs and ATs typically run at clock speeds of 8 mhz to 12 mhz. The latest Intel CPU chips (the ones used in IBMs and compatibles) are the 80386 and 80486. These run at speeds comparable to the 68030.

How long it takes the computer to do something useful, like add magenta to an image and redisplay it on the screen, also depends on the width of the data paths inside the computer. The original IBM PC used an eight-bit CPU and eight-bit data paths. IBM AT-class computers have sixteen-bit CPUs, but only eight-bit data paths. Later IBM models, such as the 386sx, match sixteen-bit CPUs with sixteen-bit data paths, and the PS/2 series finally paired a thirty-two bit processor with thirty-two bit data paths.

The Macintosh Plus and SE have thirty-two bit data paths, but only a sixteen-bit CPU. The Macintosh SE/30, II, IIx, IIcx, IIci, and IIfx are all true thirty-two bit machines, having data paths that pass thirty-two bits of data at once *and* thirty-two bit CPUs.

The efficiency of a computer's operating system and of specific software programs have a major effect on how fast the computer performs its tasks. But, given two machines with identical operating systems, software, and peripherals, the faster CPU would save you time—and frustration—when performing complex tasks.

If you're currently doing things traditionally, even a Macintosh Plus will seem like a wonder to you. But give it six months. It's like driving a car on the highway. If you accelerate from zero to sixty in eight seconds, you feel like you're flying. After an hour or two, however, you get accustomed to the speed, and sixty feels like a crawl. You want to go faster.

The same thing happens with computers. Initially, even a Mac Plus will outperform you, as you'll be splitting your time between thinking about the project you're working on and thinking about which button to push next.

As the operation of the computer becomes second nature to you, however, you'll find yourself idle as you wait for the computer to redraw complex illustrations or to re-image long blocks of text. In six months, you'll be able to manipu-

late page layouts faster than a Mac SE or a Mac II can revise them. Color—which at least triples the amount of data the computer has to digest—slows down even the speedy IIx, IIcx, and IIci machines. The era of instant response, desktop computers able to revise and display photographic color images as fast as you can issue commands, is still quite a few years away.

If you don't plan to get into complex page layouts, PostScript illustrations, or color, a basic CPU may be a good place to start. However, if your aim is to fully integrate a graphics computer with your work, we strongly recommend a model that offers both a speedy CPU and expansion slots; that means an SE/30 or one of the Macintosh II family.

### Machines For The Future

Another argument for buying an advanced, rather than a basic CPU, is the expectation that machines that are slightly second-class today will be greatly inferior before you get them paid for. The advanced CPUs should keep you at the forward edge of computing power at least long enough to pay off the loan.

The line between the upper end of the desktop computer spectrum and minicomputers is already blurred. Technologists have coined a new phrase to describe the more powerful desktop machines, such as the Macintosh II family and the IBM machines based on the 80386/486 CPUs. They call them "work stations," a term traditionally used to describe high-performance terminals used by architects and engineers to make complex technical drawings of buildings and machine parts. Desktop computers already approach some minicomputers in raw processing power. You can expect that trend to continue. The way of the future seems to be linking a number of powerful desktop units together in a network. Being linked in a network, they're able to share mass storage devices (such as optical disks) and expensive printers with the other desktop units. Some desktop networks even include a minicomputer, such as a Digital Equipment VAX. These are used to speed up data-intensive tasks such as manipulating large photographic color images.

This means you can buy into these upper-end desktop machines without worrying about obsolescence. They will become outmoded at some point; but with the capabilities of internal expansion and adding bigger processors to the network later, there's little chance that they'll become dinosaurs until long after you've recouped your initial investment.

### Family Matters

As if figuring out which CPU you need isn't enough, there are more decisions to be made about the peripherals. It's sort of like buying a car á lá carte, matching an engine with a chassis, body, interior, and ornaments. It's time consuming, but it's important. The various pieces of a graphics computer are like a family—if they're going to help and support each other, they need to get along. You might think that the computer manufacturers and software developers would make sure their gizmos will talk to and work with everyone else's gizmos. Wrong.

This is another area in which Apple has an advantage over IBM. The IBM designs are "open"; a lot of engineering details (such as the format for screen displays) were purposely left undefined so other companies could contribute their own ideas. That has happened. There are more choices of hardware in the IBM world than the Apple world. In theory, that sounds like a good thing. In practice, it leads to a whole lot of confusion. In 1988 we worked on the start-up of *PC Computing* magazine. About a dozen IBM-compatible machines from a variety of manufac-

turers were ordered for the staff. When they arrived, only two machines out of the dozen would read each other's disks! The problem was eventually solved after a number of telephone calls to the manufacturers and some adjustments to the drive units. Ironically, data format for disks is something the manufacturers all *agree* on. When you get into screen display cards, add-on memory chips, printers, and other peripherals—which they don't agree on—there are almost as many different solutions as there are manufacturers. Many of the accelerator cards, add-in RAM cards, and other accessories just won't talk to each other.

That doesn't happen often with Apple equipment. Apple sets standards for both hardware and software that are so rigid they have been accused of "terrorizing" others into following them. The result has been that, if a program or piece of hardware says "Macintosh compatible," it probably is. There were some compatibility problems in 1987 when Apple switched from the 68000 CPU used in the Plus to the 68020 CPU used in the Mac II. No one knows yet what effect Apple's next operating system (v7.0) will have on compatibility. The effect on the Mac II line and the SE/30 should be minimal.

For the other members of the family, the peripherals, the questions are mostly about speed and power.

*Accelerators:* Accelerators are circuit boards that plug into an expansion slot or into the socket for the main CPU. They make the computer work faster by increasing the clock speed of the CPU or replacing it with a faster chip, by adding RAM memory, or by adding chips to help with the arithmetic needed to draw images on a computer screen. Accelerators can help older models, such as the SE or Mac II, perform like the newer SE/30 or IIci. And they can make the newer models process big files—such as color photographs or color illustrations—faster.

*Monitors:* There are three basic types of monitors: monochrome, color, and grayscale. Monochrome monitors display black and white. Grayscale monitors display up to 256 shades of gray. The lower-priced color monitors display 256 colors simultaneously, while more expensive models display 700,000 colors simultaneously from a palette of 16.7 million. Monitor systems (a CRT and a display card) that display 256 colors are called eight-bit color systems, while the others are called twenty-four bit or thirty-two bit systems. (See *Reference And Resources*, page 151 for more information ).

The size of the monitor is critical. Get as large a monitor as you can afford. Unless you don't plan to do much more than simple page layout, we strongly recommend a monitor that measures more than sixteen inches diagonally. A sixteen-inch monitor lets you view two letter-sized pages side by side. With a smaller monitor, you'll spend an inordinate amount of time scrolling the image up, down, left, and right. When you're working on a large PostScript illustration or a multi-page document, it can be like trying to empty a bucket with a teaspoon. The screen just doesn't show enough.

*Disks:* A 40 mb disk is the minimum for a graphics computer. We have more than 20 mb of software programs alone. The electronic files for this book totaled more than 12 mb, and there are comparatively few illustrations. A single grayscale scan can take up 300 kb; ten of them equal 3 mb. A 60 mb to 100 mb disk is preferable. There are also hard disks that can store up to 45 mb on removable cartridges. When one cartridge fills up, you take it out and put in an empty one. These have become something of a standard in the design business. They allow you to pack very large files onto a portable cartridge and take it from computer to computer or to a service bureau easily. You can keep big projects organized one to a disk, and they make great devices for keeping back-up files and archives. In early 1990, they sold for less than $1,000.

*Printers:* As this book was going to press, a wave of new products was dramatically lowering prices on printers for graphics computers. PostScript laser printers—the standard against which laser printers are measured—are more expensive than printers that don't understand PostScript. PostScript is the language used by PageMaker®, Illustrator®, XPress®, and many other graphics programs to form images. It's the language used by high-resolution imagesetters to produce reproduction-quality type. PostScript laser printers cost upwards of $4,500 in 1987; by 1990, PostScript printers were available for less than $2,500.

PostScript printers allow you to use the widest variety of fonts and also allow you to print graphics from Illustrator, FreeHand®, and other PostScript programs. Non-PostScript printers don't. Software interpreters that translate PostScript commands for non-PostScript printers are available, but the ones being sold in 1990 printed pages extremely slowly; too slowly for a studio that works under tight deadlines.

Printers that use imaging models other than PostScript—such as the Hewlett-Packard Desk Jet or the GCC Technologies Personal Laser Printer—have gained some popularity. However, for serious graphics work, they still can't compete with a true PostScript machine. Several manufacturers, including Hewlett-Packard, have released PostScript interfaces to that allow some of their non-PostScript printers to understand PostScript commands.

Because the technology is changing so rapidly, we can't do much more than help you ask questions. You need a printer with PostScript capability, whether that capability comes from a separate interface or even from a software interpreter. Ask what fonts—specific brands—the printer will print. You want one that will print all

Adobe Type 1 and Type 3 fonts (assuming that the distinction between Type 1 and Type 3 fonts still exists when you read this). In 1988, Apple and Microsoft conspired to muddy the already turbid waters of the font market by announcing they were developing a new kind of font—to be called Royal fonts—that would work on both IBM and Apple computers. At the time of publication, the Royal technology was scheduled to be included in Apple's System 7.0 release.

Ask what the resolution of the printer is in dots per inch. Until 1989, the standard for laser printers was 300 dpi (dots per inch). However, some manufacturers have released laser printers or controller boards for laser printers that boost resolution as high as 1000 dpi. That's pretty close to the lowest resolution of the Linotronic 100 and Linotronic 300 imagesetters, which produce output at 1270 dpi and 2450 dpi. That means you can get output from a desktop printer on plain paper that's *almost* as good as you can get from an imagesetter. Almost, but not quite. For relatively undemanding print material, a 1000 dpi printer *might* be a viable substitute for imagesetter output.

At this time, the page size of these high-resolution laser printers is limited to 8½ x 11 inches, though models that will print on 11 x 17 paper can't be too far behind. One drawback is that the plastic ink used in laser printers is nowhere near as fine as the silver granules used in the RC paper printed by imagesetters. In the samples we've seen, small type, italic type, and reverse type set on a 1000 dpi laser printer suffered by comparison to imagesetter output. But that could change rapidly. Hewlett-Packard has released a 300 dpi laser printer capable of printing variable-sized dots, instead of uniform, square pixels. A 1000 dpi laser with this feature might come close to matching an imagesetter in type quality. At 1990 prices, these 1000 dpi laser printers cost about $8,000. Assuming you could

set all of your type on one of these printers, you can still buy a lot of type set on an imagesetter (about 1,000 pages) for that money. If you crank out high volumes of software manuals, educational materials, or retail ads, a high-resolution laser might make sense for you.

*Image scanners:* We recommend some type of image scanner for every design studio. You'll need it to make positioning images and to import sketches or photographs you want to use as the basis for illustrations or logos.

There are four types of scanners and three grades. The types are: handheld, sheetfed, flatbed, and video. The three grades are one-bit (monochrome), grayscale, and color.

Handheld scanners are about the size of a handheld waxer. They are perfectly adequate for importing small sketches. Most are monochrome, which means they only capture images as black or white with no grays. Some come with software that "dithers" this high-contrast image, simulating shades of gray. At 1990 prices, handheld scanners cost $300-$600.

To use a sheetfed scanner, you put a sheet of paper into a slot where a roller grabs it and runs it over the scanning sensor. Sheetfed scanners can be monochrome or grayscale. In most sheetfed scanners, the paper tends to skew one way or the other while going through, resulting in an image that's slightly off the vertical. It can be annoying to have to rotate these images before placing them in a layout. At 1990 prices, sheetfed scanners cost $600 to $1,200.

Flatbed scanners work like a xerographic copying machine. You place the piece to be scanned on a sheet of glass on the top of the scanner, square it up, close the cover, and scan. Flatbed scanners can be monochrome, grayscale, or color.

These handheld, sheetfed, and flatbed scanners weren't designed to scan transparencies. If you often use 35mm slides or other color transparencies in your work, you'll have to either buy a color slide scanner ($4,500 to $12,000) or invent your way around the problem.

One solution is to buy a backlight unit, such as the one sold by the Izumiya Company. The light box can be used to illuminate a transparency from behind, so that a photocopier or flatbed scanner can capture the image. Some other things that work, but which are a lot of trouble are: using a photographic enlarger and a Polaroid film back from a studio camera or a Polaroid slide printer (about $100, from Polaroid) to make prints; and using a slide-copier device to copy the slides onto color or black and white print film.

Video scanners are an alternative. Several manufacturers sell devices (called digitizers) that convert video signals to files that can be read and used by graphics computers. In 1990, they ranged in price from $300 to $1,000. Even the lowest-priced models capture grayscale images. Some also capture color images.

To get an image into the scanner, you'll need a video signal from a video camera or a video-cassette recorder. We use a black and white security camera made by RCA (the same kind that watch you in drug stores) and a MacVision digitizer. By mounting the camera on a copy stand designed for 35mm cameras (about $50 at a camera supply store), you can point it straight down and adjust its height easily. Mount the copy stand to a light table. Place the transparencies on the light table, turn on the camera, and presto, a slide scanner. You may need an adapter, called a macro tube or macro adapter, to get the camera lens to focus close enough to fill up the video frame with a 35mm slide. These adapters are available through camera supply stores that cater to the film or video trade.

Still video cameras, which look a lot like 35mm cameras but use a magnetic disk to record still video frames instead of traditional film, may be an alternative as well. Check with a camera store for prices and models.

The resolution of most video cameras can't match the resolution of a flatbed scanner, so video images aren't as sharp and crisp as images from a flatbed scanner. High-resolution video cameras are available, but they cost even more than the expensive slide scanners. However, a home video camera or security-grade camera can provide perfectly adequate positioning images. The camera also allows you to scan in three-dimensional objects, a plus if you use live objects as the basis for illustrations. If your work requires great precision, get a video camera with a CCD (Charge Coupled Device) pickup instead of a vidicon tube. The tubes tend to distort objects slightly when they heat up. With the digitizer and camera plus a light table, copy stand, and macro adapter, you can put together a slide scanner for less than $1,000.

***Extra RAM:*** For now, you can get by with 1 mb RAM if you intend to do simple page layout. If you want to do PostScript illustrations, complex page layout, or work with photographs, the minimum is 2 mb, and 4 mb is preferred. If you intend to design in color, plan on 4 mb minimum, with 8 mb being the preferred set-up. At 1990 prices, RAM cost about $90 per megabyte. Don't squawk; in 1988, RAM chips cost $300 per megabyte *if* you could find them.

Not all RAM is created equal. The speed with which it can write or read data is measured in nanoseconds, abbreviated ns. The lower the number, the faster the RAM. Naturally, the faster CPU chips work best with faster RAM chips. Buy the fastest RAM chips available. In 1990, those were 70ns chips.

RAM chips fit into the Macintosh in a not-too-obvious and regimented way. There's no way to install 3 mb RAM, for example. The choices are 1, 2, 4, 5, or 8 mb. Consider having a dealer do this upgrade for you.

## Software Selector

Choosing software can be frustrating; just when you think you know everything about a group of competing programs, a new program or major upgrade changes the picture. Take it for granted that you'll never have all of the information you need to make an informed choice, but the chart at right will get you started with a basic tool kit of programs.

### Price Matters Here, Too

We generally don't recommend buying the lowest-priced program in any category. And just because a package has a high price tag doesn't mean it's the best in its field. The leading programs in each category are often similar in their abilities, but they can differ significantly in how they operate. The distinctions often come down to which program makes you most comfortable.

The way to compare programs is to talk to people who do work similar to yours. Test drive before you buy. Try the software out at a computer dealer or on a rental machine at a desktop publishing service bureau. Some mail-order suppliers will rent programs for two weeks; however, the fees they charge for top-rated programs ($40 to $75) are high. Most deduct the rental fee from the purchase price if you decide to buy the program after the rental period. You can find their ads in the computer magazines.

There's nothing more frustrating than working with an inadequate software package. It doesn't make sense to cripple a $10,000 computer system by feeding it inadequate software that saved you a couple of hundred dollars.

Not all the packages you buy are going to work. Taking that as a given, judge the risk of any given software package by its price. We don't spend a lot of time investigating packages that cost under $200. If the reviews say it will fulfill a need we have, we'll try it. So far, we've bought about $1,000 worth of software that's marginally useful, at best. If you're on a tight budget, try the program before buying or buy from a mail order source that will guarantee the product's performance. In 1989, several larger mail-order firms began underwriting selected software, offering a thirty-day money back guarantee if the program didn't live up to your expectations.

When it comes to choosing core programs—page layout and illustration—experience is the best guide. Again, try them before you buy.

While word processing and page layout software have only a slight effect on your creative options, illustration packages are like different paintbrushes: Each one has its own style and creates a limited number of visual effects. If you only learn and use one program, your style will be limited by the software. The tool will be controlling you, instead of you controlling the tool. The point of the computer as a design tool is to *expand* your creative options, not limit them. For that reason, we'd recommend that you buy several illustration programs: Illustrator, FreeHand, Canvas®, *and* PixelPaint®, for example.

A good way to start out is with a "basic" tool kit of software, adapted to the kind of work you do. You can then budget $1,000 or so annually to add to your tool kit. Every other month, investigate and purchase a new program.

Don't scrimp on fonts. Even though you're going to get thirty-five fonts when you buy a PostScript printer, you'll need many more unless your work is very repetitive. One way to beat the high cost of fonts is to buy from vendors other than Adobe. In 1989, Image Club began offering a compact disk with 600 fonts on it called Type Vendor. The disk was priced at $199 with 20 fonts unlocked and ready to use. To access other fonts, Image Club charged $10 to $20 per font for an access code. If you didn't have a compact disk reader, Image Club also offered the fonts on a floppy disk for about $25 each.

This chart is only a guide. You're the only one who knows what you want to accomplish, how much new equipment your studio is capable of absorbing, and how heavily you will rely on the computers. For each of the tasks, we've keyed the chart to show what programs you must have, pieces that are strongly recommended, and pieces that are optional. In each case the "must have" packages are those that are essential; you can't get the job done effectively without them. The "strongly recommended" software will increase productivity or enhance your capability in that area. "Optional" programs are extremely useful, but not critical.

Key: M: Must have  S: Strongly recommend  O: Optional

| | Word Process | Page Layout | Fonts | Font Creation | Drawing | Imaging | Retouch | Spread-sheet | Graph | Presen-tation | Commu-nication | CAD | Billing/Account | Utilities |
|---|---|---|---|---|---|---|---|---|---|---|---|---|---|---|
| **Stage One** | | | | | | | | | | | | | | |
| Type design/selection | M | M | M | O | | | | | | | | | | |
| Rough layouts | | M | M | O | | | | | | | | | | |
| Comps | | M | M | O | | | | | | | | | | |
| Repro Type | | M | M | O | | | | | | | | | | |
| Mechanical art | | M | M | O | | S | O | | O | | | | | |
| **Stage Two** | | | | | | | | | | | | | | |
| Conceptual design | | S | M | S | M | M | O | | | | S | O | | S |
| Positioning images | | M | | | | M | M | | | | | | | S |
| Illustrations | | S | | S | M | M | S | | O | | | S | | S |
| Film negatives | | S | | | | | | | | | | | | |
| Spot color separations | | S | | | S | | | | | | | | | |
| Slides | | | M | | M | S | O | | S | M | | O | | |
| Logotypes | | | M | M | M | S | O | | | | | | | S |
| Telecommunications | M | | | | | | | | | | M | | | S |
| Estimating | | | | | | | | M | | | | | S | |
| Scheduling/Tracking | | | | | | | | S | | | | | M | |
| **Stage Three** | | | | | | | | | | | | | | |
| Photo imaging/separation | | S | | | | M | M | | | | | | | S |
| Full color computer design | | M | M | | M | M | M | | S | | S | O | | S |
| Video | | | | S | M | M | M | | | S | | | | |
| Animation | | | M | S | M | S | M | | | S | | | | |
| Three-dimensional design | | | | | M | S | O | | | | | M | | |
| Billing/accounting | M | | | | | | | M | O | | | | M | |

## Utility Belt

There are dozens of small programs, called utilities, that can make life with your computer more pleasant and more convenient. At a minimum you should have a good virus checker or two, such as SAM®, or Virex®; a calendar/telephone book such as DynoDex® or Borland SideKick®; an archiving program that will compress large files for easier storage and telecommunications (Stuffit® is the most widely used); a file locator that can search your hard disk for specific files or for words within those files; possibly a conversion utility for changing graphics files from TIFF format to PICT format and back; and a font management program such as Suitcase II® or Master Juggler®.

This is the time you've been dreading; time to put your wish list on paper and find out how bad it's going to hurt your wallet. The good news is that you do have choices, and it's possible to build a system slowly without getting locked into obsolete hardware.

Since the major software programs tend to evolve, as a registered user, you'll be able to receive upgrades as the programs are improved. We started using Quark XPress® with version 1.0 in 1987; since then the program has gone through at least six major upgrades, averaging one every six months. Some manufacturers charge a small fee for their upgrades, while others offer an "extended warranty." You pay a set amount per year and receive all upgrades released during that time. You won't be able to upgrade your software if you use someone else's copy instead of buying your own. Using unlicensed software is illegal (it's called "piracy"). It violates the software developer's copyright on the program. If you use pirated software, you won't be able to get copies of the manuals and you won't be able to get technical support, which is very important for complex software.

It's always hazardous to tell someone else how to run their business, but we're going to plunge in anyway and make some specific recommendations. Keep in mind that these were written early in 1990, and that by the time you read this, there may well be better options available. The prices will almost certainly have changed. The three buying strategies are offered as examples of how to build a system and the types of basic building blocks you'll need at each step in your evolution.

By now you should be reading the ads in the computer magazines closely and understanding a lot of what you see. Use these buying strategies to make a trial system list for yourself. Check the pricing by matching your list against prices listed in the mail order ads.

### Stage One: Getting Your Feet Wet

This is the soft, slow start. It will let you get a taste of most of the benefits of a graphics computer system without having to stake the future of your business or your financial well-being on how well it works.

*You:* A small studio, solo practitioner, in-house communications department, or student looking for a way to boost your creativity, your productivity, and ultimately your profit.

*Your work:* One- and two-color brochures, letterhead designs, newsletters, retail ads.

*Your clients:* Small local firms who demand a lot but don't want to pay too much, perhaps a local hospital or trade association office.

*Your needs:* Typesetting, rough layouts, and simple mechanical art.

### Hardware
Basic system

| | |
|---|---|
| Macintosh SE | $ 1,900 |
| PostScript printer | 2,400 |
| 60 mb hard disk drive | 700 |
| *Subtotal* | *$ 5,000* |

### Extended system, add:

| | |
|---|---|
| Upgrade to Macintosh SE/30 | $ 1,000 |
| Two-page display | 900 |
| 2.5 mb RAM | 200 |
| Extended keyboard | 140 |
| Handheld scanner | 350 |
| *Subtotal* | *$ 2,590* |

### Software:

| | |
|---|---|
| Page layout | $ 500 |
| Five additional font packages | 650 |
| Word processing | 100 |
| Utilities | 250 |
| *Subtotal* | *$ 1,500* |

*Basic system plus software* .............. *$ 6,500*
*Extended system plus software* ...... *$ 9,090*

## Stage Two: Power Up

You're already sure you want to play, but need a place to start.

*You:* A studio with two to five designers, a solo practitioner, or communications department

*Your work:* Four-color brochures, logos, books and complex publications, illustrations.

*Your clients:* Regional and national firms who expect top quality results.

*Your needs:* Complex mechanicals, PostScript illustrations, presentations, controls for your own business.

### Hardware

| | |
|---|---|
| Basic system | |
| Macintosh SE/30 | |
| with 4 mb RAM, 80mb disk | $ 4,000 |
| PostScript printer | 2,400 |
| Extended keyboard | 140 |
| Two page monitor | 900 |
| *Subtotal* | *$ 7,440* |

### Extended system, add:

| | |
|---|---|
| Upgrade to Mac IIcx CPU, add | $ 400 |
| Flatbed scanner, grayscale | 1,450 |
| Additional 256-color monitor | 1,200 |
| 45 mb removable cartridge drive | 900 |
| *Subtotal* | *$ 3,950* |

### Software:

| | |
|---|---|
| Page layout | $ 500 |
| Ten additional font packages | 1,500 |
| Word processing | 100 |
| Utilities | 250 |
| Illustration | 600 |
| Imaging | 250 |
| Font manipulation | 150 |
| Spreadsheet | 250 |
| *Subtotal* | *$ 3,600* |

| | |
|---|---|
| *Basic system plus software* | *$ 11,040* |
| *Extended system plus software* | *$ 14,990* |

## Stage Three: Maximum Macs

After some experience, you'll be ready for a system that will let you tackle anything.

*You:* A large studio, publishing company, communications department, advertising agency.

*Your work:* Packaging, annual reports, four-color brochures, logos, books and complex publications, illustrations, posters.

*Your clients:* Fortune 500 and other large regional and national firms.

*Your needs:* Knock-'em-dead presentations and comps, complex mechanicals, full-color design on the screen, PostScript illustrations, tight financial controls for your own business.

### Hardware

| | |
|---|---|
| Macintosh IIci | $ 4,700 |
| 8 mb RAM | 1,000 |
| PostScript printer | 5,000 |
| Color printer | 8,000 |
| Extended keyboard | 140 |
| Color/grayscale scanner | 2,000 |
| Photographic color monitor | 4,500 |
| 100 mb hard disk | 1,100 |
| 45 mb removable cartridge drive | 900 |
| *Subtotal* | *$ 27,340* |

### Software:

| | |
|---|---|
| Page layout | $ 500 |
| Forty additional font packages | 8,000 |
| Word processing | 100 |
| Utilities | 450 |
| Illustration | 1,200 |
| Imaging | 1,000 |
| Font manipulation | 750 |
| Spreadsheet | 250 |
| Presentation | 300 |
| 3-D and CAD drawing | 1,000 |
| Billing/Accounting | 750 |
| *Subtotal* | *$ 14,300* |

| | |
|---|---|
| *Hardware/software total* | *$ 41,640* |

## Penny-Pinching Production

Not everyone wants—or *needs*—a full-bore TurboMax 76000-X with a 90 mhz accelerator, six gigabyte floppy-optical jukebox, thirty-two bit color display/digitizer card, and a lime green LED panel the size of a Chrysler mini-van that flashes the lyrics to *Figaro* while displaying news, weather, and World Soccer League scores.

Maybe all you need is a modest system, something that will do lightweight page layout that's also light on your budget.

### The Lower-Priced Spread

You can realize a large share of the purely economic benefits of a graphics computer with a small investment. How does $3,500 sound? A basic system—a modest CPU, a printer, and a page layout program—can save you a bundle on typesetting. We're not talking about illustrations or designing three-dimensional logos. We're just talking about setting type. By doing your own keyboarding and running the type as straight galleys, you can get enough type to fill a letter-sized page for $8. Unless your client supplies copy to you on a computer disk, you'll have to type it in or pay someone to type it for you. You'll also have to paste it up, unless you send it to the service bureau in page make-up form (in which case the type will cost you $8 per finished page instead of $8 per galley).

If you're not interested in turning your business into a digital design studio, or just want to crank out some low-intensity print graphics, this is an adequate solution. You could add a mid-priced drawing program (such as McDraw II® or Canvas) to make simple illustrations. Most service bureaus have scanners and will scan photographs for you at a reasonable price.

At this level, an IBM AT-compatible CPU is a possible choice. If you already have an IBM-compatible, use it in lieu of a Macintosh. All you'll need is a page layout program, a laser or ink-jet printer, and possibly a new display card and monitor (roughly $2,000 total). If you don't already own an IBM-compatible computer, the Macintosh Plus, which in 1990 was selling for $1,200 new and well under $1,000, is probably a better choice. It's easier to learn and use. It also gives you the choice of upgrading to a more elaborate Macintosh system later, carrying with you the software and printer you've already purchased. The Plus could then be used as a spare machine or as a semi-portable if you sometimes take work home or work in someone else's office.

At early 1990 prices, the cost of these two systems would be:

### IBM Based System

| | |
|---|---|
| IBM AT-compatible computer | $ 1,400 |
| Laser printer | 1,400 |
| Page layout software | 450 |
| **Total** | **$ 3,250** |

### Macintosh System

| | |
|---|---|
| Macintosh Plus | $ 1,200 |
| 40 mb disk drive | 450 |
| Laser printer | 1,400 |
| Page layout software | 450 |
| **Total** | **$ 3,500** |

The things you're not getting with these packages are legion: illustration, positioning images, the ability to produce and render complex designs and logos. And you won't get much of a boost creatively from these systems.

The other thing you won't get is a lot of debt. If you find that you like the computer, if it works its way into your daily routine and you find yourself becoming an addict, you can always use these low-end systems as a launching point. In the meantime, you'll be learning some programs and saving money.

# Chapter Eight:
# Ante Up: How To Pay The Piper

**Leases/Loans**

**Insurance**

## Leases/Loans

Unless you're in a position to run down to your local computer dealer and write a check for upwards of $7,000, you need to think about how you're going to pay for your system—leasing or a business loan. You'll have interest costs, of course, but at least the system expense can be deducted from your income.

### Leave Me A Loan!

One option is to use your credit cards to finance your system. A lot of solo practitioners and small studios do this, but the interest rates on credit cards are very high—five to seven percentage points above the prime lending rate is not uncommon. On a $10,000 loan for thirty-six months, every point above prime will cost you approximately $175 over the term of the loan. Five points is $875 in extra interest, the price of a two-page monitor.

A better option might be to apply for a secured loan at your bank, where you'll pay two to three points above the prime rate. You may be able to use the equipment itself as collateral for the loan, or the bank might ask you to pledge other collateral. If you already have a credit line at your bank, and there's plenty of elbow room to handle both your cash flow needs *and* the price of a system, this is probably the least expensive financing.

### Leasing

There are advantages to leasing, rather than making an outright purchase. For one, it doesn't draw on your other sources of credit, credit you may need to cover operating expenses. Banks typically don't care to take business equipment as collateral for loans, though they may make the loan if you pledge your personal assets to guarantee it. Leasing companies, especially those set up by dealers or manufacturers, are happy to use the equipment to secure the lease. Another plus is that, if you lease through a dealer or manufacturer, they may offer you the option of upgrading the equipment during the lease. This arrangement will allow you to trade in your used gear and trade up to newer equipment as your needs change.

There are two types of leases—operating leases and financial leases. In an operating lease, you agree to pay a certain number of monthly payments for a certain period of time. At the end of that time, the equipment can be sold to you at a fair market value. This is typically 10 percent of the original purchase price. A financial lease is really a form of installment loan. In it, you agree to make payments as with an operating lease, but the lease includes a provision that allows you to buy the equipment for a specific amount of money (as opposed to a percentage of market value) at the end of the lease.

If you take out an operating lease, you will be able to deduct the payments from your income as an expense item; equipment acquired through outright purchase or a financial lease must be depreciated, with a portion of the purchase price deducted in each of five or seven years.

The line between operating leases and financial leases is thin and shadowy, at best. Leasing companies often offer what they purport to be an operating lease, but provide a way for you to acquire the equipment for a very small payment at the end of the lease. If the Internal Revenue Service determines that the "buy out" payment is not based on the fair market value of the equipment, it could rule the lease a financial lease and make you change the structure of your deductions. Before leasing equipment, talk to a qualified accountant about the rules for deducting equipment costs and, if possible, show him a copy of the lease you're considering.

To start a lease, you'll usually pay a small security deposit (usually one or two monthly

## Lease Rates And Payment Schedules

Leasing rates, like all finance rates, are almost as changeable as the weather. These calculations were made based on the assumption that the prime lending rate was 10 percent. Naturally, if that rate rises, the amount of interest paid over the life of a lease would increase and the payments would go up. Also, changes in the way leasing companies are allowed to write off depreciation and other market factors could cause interest charges and fees associated with leases to change.

| Cost Of System | Monthly Payments 48 Month Lease | Total Of Payments | Interest Charged |
|---|---|---|---|
| $ 4,000 | $ 113 | $ 5,400 | $ 1,400 |
| 5,000 | 141 | 6,750 | 1,750 |
| 7,500 | 210 | 10,125 | 2,625 |
| 10,000 | 281 | 13,500 | 3,500 |
| 15,000 | 422 | 20,250 | 5,250 |
| 20,000 | 563 | 27,000 | 7,000 |

payments) and the first month's payment. A bank will likely require you to make a down payment equal to 25 percent of the equipment's purchase price.

There are drawbacks to leases, too. You'll probably have to pay top dollar for the equipment. Your power to bargain the seller's price down will be compromised considerably if you're asking him to loan you the money to make the purchase. Also, if you want to end a lease early, you'll get hammered. In a sixty month lease, for example, you typically don't start making any payments against the purchase price of the equipment until after three years. It's possible to make monthly payments for three years, then find out you still owe the leasing company a large part of the original retail value

of the equipment. If you want to get out of the lease, you'll have to pay them the difference between the balance on the lease and the actual current value of the equipment. That difference could be substantial.

While leasing is a legitimate and useful business service, there are less-than-scrupulous companies who find that the general public's lack of knowledge about leases affords them the opportunity to make additional profits. If you're considering a lease, get a copy of the lease agreement and have your accountant or attorney review it. Is there a "commitment fee" written into the lease? A commitment fee is any amount the leasing company asks for as a guarantee before processing your lease application. Make absolutely certain that any money you pay to a leasing company before you sign the actual lease document is refundable. In some cases, leasing companies do charge a small non-refundable fee to cover the cost of checking your credit, but this shouldn't exceed $50. Verify for yourself that the lease application states clearly that any advance fee is refundable if for any reason the lease is denied or the vendor is unable to deliver the equipment.

Read the lease carefully and make sure you understand who's responsible for the maintenance. Usually, the operator (you) is responsible for keeping the equipment in working order. Occasionally, especially if the leasing company or vendor is heavily involved in the computer market, a service contract will be included in the lease price. Generally, though, the leasing company is just a broker, and they don't guarantee that the equipment will be suitable for your business or that it will work. If you have a problem with the equipment, you can't just stop making payments and give it back to the leasing company. They have the right to come after your business assets if you fail to make the payments. If you're a small studio or have been in operation less than two years, it's highly likely that the leasing company, like the bank, will require that you guarantee the lease personally. If anything goes wrong, that gives them the right to sue you, not your business.

### Making Sure With Insurance

Your standard business insurance may not cover theft or damage to computer equipment. It almost certainly won't cover electrical damage caused by power fluctuations. If it does cover the equipment for theft, it probably pays only a reduced "market value" for the equipment. Computers depreciate quickly. If you lease a $15,000 system, after two years of payments, you might still owe $12,000 on it. If it were stolen, it's likely the insurance company would offer you $7,500 or less. That leaves you without your equipment and $4,500 short of paying off the lease so you can replace it.

Safeware, an insurance company headquartered in Columbus, Ohio, insures computers for their full *replacement* value, plus they'll insure your software and even data disks. The policy will pay you if the equipment is damaged by a voltage surge or voltage drop caused by your power company. Their rates are reasonable and the service we've gotten from them has been superb. The address is listed in *Reference And Resources*, page 151, and Safeware advertises frequently in the computer magazines.

### Planning Ahead

However you finance your system, don't think of the initial purchase price as the total price. With the exception of the most expensive (stage three) system, we specified only the minimum hardware and software. There are other pieces you'll need immediately, such as a good surge protector ($100), a mouse pad ($10), disks ($14 per box), and cables to connect your computer to the printer ($25 to $95). Other, more expensive, items that you now consider frills will become necessities in a matter of months.

Your initial purchase is the first step on a path that is as long as your pockets are deep. Unless you have a very specific, closed-ended task for the computer, its uses (and its total cost) will expand as you become more proficient.

Leave a little extra room in your budget—$500—for incidentals during the first two months you own the system. After your budget has had time to recuperate, plan to spend $50 to $150 a month (for a stage one system) or $200 to $300 a month (for a stage two system) on building your font library and upgrading hardware and software.

# Section III:
# Making It All Pay Off

**113  Chapter Nine:**
**Integrating People And Processes**

**121  Chapter Ten: The Well-Trained Studio**

**125  Chapter Eleven:**
**Working With A Service Bureau**

**131  Chapter Twelve:**
**Managing A Computer System**

**137  Chapter Thirteen:**
**Things That Can—And Will—Go Wrong**

**141  Chapter Fourteen: Business Class**

**147  Chapter Fifteen: Heading For A Far Horizon**

**151  Chapter Sixteen: Reference And Resources**

# Chapter Nine:
# Integrating People And Processes

**Integrating Your Computer:**
**Possibilities And Procedures**

**Procedure Check**

**Hornall Anderson Design Works /**
**Glasgow & Associates**

**Ziff-Davis Publishing Company/**
**Blount & Walker Visual Communications**

**Future Studio: Mark Crumpacker**

New tools require new procedures; you need to think carefully about how work will flow in and through your studio. The chart (opposite) reflects a fundamental difference in how traditional studios operate versus how work flows though a studio that has fully integrated a graphics computer.

The change designers say is most dramatic is in the control—of quality, of timing—that not having to wait for typesetters and photostat houses gives them. It shortens the production phase of their process and improves it. Those changes may require some getting used to.

Initially, most designers use the computer as simply a typesetter and electronic drafting board. They conceptualize, as they always have, with a sketch pad and perhaps use computer type in their roughs, but don't really commit projects to the computer until it's time to make presentation boards or, even later, mechanicals. While it's perfectly acceptable to fit the computer into your existing process, the greatest rewards come to those who adapt their way of working to take advantage of the computer's unique ability to *reduce* the number of steps in the design and production process.

Require your clients to submit copy to you on disk as early as possible—before you make presentation boards, if possible.

Get copywriters into the design process early by giving them word counts after you've done thumbnails but before you create computer roughs or presentation boards.

Set up your agreements so that client approvals can be made in one step. Don't have them approve a rough, then write copy, get a sign-off on the copy, then show the copy in a layout. Instead put the actual copy into the rough layout so they approve both at once. This eliminates one full round of revisions.

Don't show too many alternative designs at once. The client may get the idea that, now that you have a graphics computer, it's "no big deal" for you to whip out another dozen concepts. You can, of course, do this much faster with a computer, but unless they're willing to pay for your time, they shouldn't ask for endless rounds of new concepts.

Similarly, one advantage of the computer is that you don't set—and pay for—type until everything's perfect. Some clients may take that as permission for them to keep adjusting copy and layout. Typesetters charge for author's alterations; you have the right to do that also. The revisions may again seem like no big deal to a client, but they *are* a big deal because the labor required to make them comes out of your fee.

When you do send a file to type, make certain that it's actually ready to go to the *printer*, because it should be a complete mechanical when it's returned. You have to let clients know that their last laser proof is actually a proof of the final mechanical.

As you gain experience, you'll find that almost anything you now do by hand can be done with a computer. However, it's not always efficient to spend the time to learn a new computer technique. If you think you might repeat the technique on another job, learn it. If it's something you're not likely to repeat, doing it by hand may save the time you'd have spent wrestling with a software manual.

Most designers still find that conceptual sketching is best done with a pad. Drawing with a computer requires a structured, technical process. Conceptualizing should be more intuitive. If you're sketching with a pencil, it's easy enough to make a line heavier to emphasize part of a design. Darkening a line with the computer requires you to think, then type on a keyboard.

Start your process with the computer as soon after the conceptual design as possible. If you do a rough on tissue paper, you'll just have to redraw it in the computer later.

The simplified diagrams below reflect one of the most important advantages of a graphics computer: You don't have to send out (and wait for) type until the end of the process.

**Traditional Process**

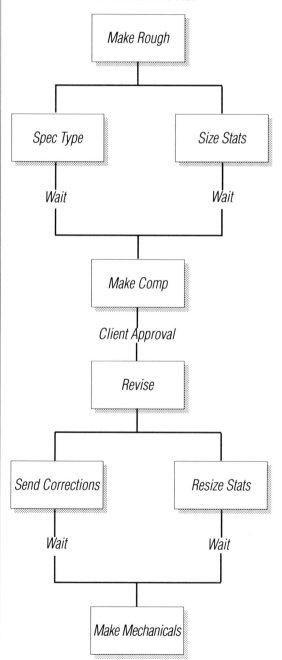

**Using A Graphics Computer**

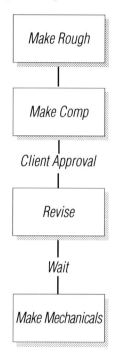

The shorter the "back end" of your process, the more time you'll have to spend on design on the front end. Alternatively, that time can be used to work on other projects, generating additional revenues or can boost your bottom line by saving labor.

Also, the fewer times you have to pause and wait for something—a response from the client or materials from an outside vendor—the shorter the process and the more control you have over your deadlines. While you may at first find that doing your own typesetting is a chore, as soon as you integrate typesetting with making the comp, you'll begin to realize an enormous reduction in the number of days it takes to get a project through the studio from sale to invoicing.

## HORNALL ANDERSON DESIGN WORKS: Easing Into The Digital World

***Brian O'Neill***
*Designer, Network Administrator*
*Hornall Anderson Design Works, Seattle*
*Eleven designers, four project managers*
*Computer graphics equipment: ten*
*Macintosh II-series CPUs with Apple color*
*monitors, five SE/30s, two SEs, one Plus, one*
*Macintosh 512E, Apple Laserwriter, Scanner*

Brian O'Neill may have made the ultimate sacrifice. The Seattle designer was a successful freelancer who often worked with Hornall Anderson Design Works, a local studio with an international reputation. The studio liked his work but they were even more intrigued with his knowledge of the Macintosh computer. Two years ago, Jack Anderson and John Hornall convinced O'Neill to take a break from his practice and install a graphics computer system at Hornall Anderson. Since then, much of his time has been taken up buying systems and training others to design on a computer, rather than designing himself.

"Jack and John didn't want to dump a lot of money into hardware until they could see whether graphics computers would work in their studio, whether they would be accepted," O'Neill recalls. "We built slowly rather than buying a lot of hardware all at once. I teach a basic course in computer graphics at a college, so we put everyone through a basic seminar in PageMaker®. At first, everyone thought the computer was terrific. When they saw that it could wrap type around a circle, or rotate things on screen, they were excited. But those feelings died down when they had to sit down and learn how to do them. They'd love to be able to produce special effects themselves, but they

say, 'Sure, you can do that because you know how. It would take me hours to do that.'

"The biggest hurdle here at Hornall Anderson has been getting them to hang in there long enough to actually sit down and use the machines.

"I've probably contributed to them *not* using the computers because we've set up a services branch. Designers can come to the services people and have them create an effect. I'd prefer that everyone know the computer well enough that we didn't have to do that. But it seems to be working."

While doing what seems to work, O'Neill has also worked hard to achieve his ideal. He produces an in-house newsletter he calls *Club Le Disc* to keep the troops motivated and share tips and techniques. Given the large size of the staff, it's also a good way to publicize information and reinforce procedures, such as conventions on naming files.

"It's controlled anarchy out there—barely controlled," O'Neill muses. In most non-studio settings, employees conform to strict standards for how they use their systems, how they save and store data, and more. Conformity is not the long suit of most designers. O'Neill backs up data files himself, moving from station to station with a 45 mb cartridge drive. O'Neill admits staying on top of the details of keeping the system running has cut into his own design projects deeply. Still, he considers the experience worthwhile.

"We've gotten to the point where we decide whether or not to do something on the computer based on whether we have a skilled Mac designer available, rather than on whether our system can handle the job," he said proudly.

## DALE GLASGOW: A Startling Illustration

*Dale Glasgow*
*Glasgow & Associates*
*Computer graphics equipment: Macintosh IIcx, Apple Laserwriter IINT, extended keyboard, 100-megabyte disk drive, 4 megabytes RAM, color monitor, flatbed scanner*

When *USA Today* was launched, it was derided by its more traditional competitors, who, likening it to a fast-food hamburger, called it "McPaper." The critics, of course, haven't kept *USA Today* from becoming a success. From its inception, one of the progressive newspaper's hallmarks has been high-quality, full-color informational graphics. These have turned the snide put-down into a journalistic "in your face." *USA Today* is indeed a "Mac Paper." The newspaper has been in the forefront of using Macintosh computers to turn out excellent illustrations under tremendous deadline pressure. One of the artists who helped make that happen was Dale Glasgow.

Glasgow has now moved into private practice. Though he still does work for *USA Today*, his client list has expanded to include *National Geographic* magazine, book publishers, and large corporate accounts.

Adept with an airbrush and a pencil, Glasgow has for several years found more of his work migrating to the Macintosh.

"I'm old enough that computers weren't even talked about as tools when I was in school. My style was pretty well set before I began working with the Macintosh. There are certain things I do, and it's a question of whether or not the machine can do them. As far as the Mac versus an airbrush, there's no comparison, at least not yet. It can't model a curve with a fade, for example, like an airbrush can. But for some things, I think it's better. If I have a simple illustration, I like using the Mac because it has type capabilities. If you have a line drawing, you can add color quickly. And sometimes clients specifically ask for Mac graphics because they want to bypass conventional separations and go straight to film, or they want to bring the illustration into their computer and modify it. It can be a hard call whether to use the Mac or reach for my airbrush."

In some cases, Glasgow uses both: "I did a piece that was very complex, a line drawing that took about fifty hours to complete. I had it output through a Linotronic onto RC paper, then used an airbrush on top of the paper."

The Mac's malleable line drawing tools and rescalable files made it a good choice for the line drawing, but the final product needed shading that's currently beyond the reach of desktop computers.

"The biggest disappointments I've had are in outputting color separation film," Glasgow said. "If you have a job that takes ten hours to run on a Linotronic and, after the negatives are done, you find a moiré, it's horrifying. You have to run the negatives again, and the illustrator can take a big hit financially. Sometimes the service bureau will re-run them at a low rate or for free. It's important to find a bureau that will work with you in good times *and* in bad or you can go broke fast."

Glasgow's wish list? Faster screen redraw for twenty-four bit color and better control over the separation process. He expects to get his wishes soon: "Progress is being made so fast, I have a hard time keeping up with it."

117

**Ziff-Davis Publishing / Blount & Walker Visual Communications**

## ZIFF-DAVIS PUBLISHING: High Volume Plus Continuous-Tone Color Separations

***Lloyd Schultz***
*Desktop Production Director*
*Ziff-Davis Publishing Company*
*Wide variety of CPUs, peripherals, software*

Lloyd Schultz could be called a designer's best friend. As production director for seven computer-related magazines, Schultz is charged with making sure the staffs have the systems to stay on time and on budget. In too many organizations, that pressure might force compromises. Schultz, however, strives hard to provide the designers with cutting-edge technology that *works*. His approach is rational and well-planned. Interestingly, he's come up with the same answers as many of the gut-reaction decision makers in design studios.

"No one in production management would do page makeup on anything *but* a Mac," Schultz said. "But they also wouldn't do word processing on anything except an IBM."

IBM's edge in word processing is largely due to one software product, XyWrite®. According to Schultz, it produces the cleanest files of any word processing package. Clean files are easier to import into a page layout program. Schultz said Quark XPress® 3.0 may change that; it's ease of use may make it *the* program of choice.

Each of the magazines uses a different combination of hardware and software. The most extensive use of desktop gear is at the Macintosh-specific magazines.

***MacWeek:*** Everything for this slick industry tabloid—including continuous-tone color separations—is produced on Macintosh equipment. Color photographs are scanned on a Nikon scanner. Most are kept to a one-column width to keep the color from falling apart

under enlargement as the originals are mostly 35mm. All editorial elements of the pages are created and positioned with a Mac. The magazine has its own Linotronic L-300 and even pulls its own color proofs using a contact frame and Chroma Check materials.

"Adobe PhotoShop is what made the color separations possible," Schultz says. "We're only pushing them at *MacWeek* because you have to do a lot of separations to justify the cost of the gear and a trained operator."

***MacUser:*** Everything except continuous-tone color photographs is created and separated using Macintosh gear at this California-based monthly. One unusual need is the "screen grab": images taken from a computer monitor to demonstrate what software programs look like while they're running. These grabs make large—up to 4 mb—files.

***Computer Shopper:*** An average one hundred ads per issue are built or modified on Macintosh using PageMaker®. The editorial pages are created in Quark XPress.

***PC Magazine:*** This IBM-specific monthly has worked for almost two years to match *MacUser*'s performance. Because it doesn't use Macintosh work stations, to date only about 20 percent of the magazine's pages are created on desktop equipment each month.

***PC Week:*** It takes eight designers to produce the one hundred-plus color graphics that appear in each weekly issue. Using Macintosh IIcx CPUs with 8 mb of RAM, they create the graphics in FreeHand®. "We haven't put accelerators on their CPUs yet," Schultz chuckles. "With that many graphics, they just smoke those Macs." The editorial pages are created on IBM PCs and the graphics stripped in manually.

*Blount & Walker Visual Communications*
*Three designers*
*Computer graphics equipment: two Macintosh II CPUs, one Plus, extended keyboards, 60-megabyte disk drives, 2 megabytes RAM, E-Machines 16-inch monitors, video and flatbed scanners, Apple Laserwriter Plus*

Our own studio has been an on-going case study in the use of desktop computer technology for publishing and graphic arts. Our decision to purchase a Macintosh system was driven by economics and by the capacity to produce repro type on a high-resolution imagesetter. But the personal motivation to apply technology to our field was sparked much earlier; in the mid-1970s when we began using early computer-driven typesetting equipment to create simple page layout files. When personal computers became available in the late 1970s, we telecommunicated galley type to typesetters. In 1982 we were using IBM compatible computers and a grotesque, user-hostile page layout program to print laser proofs in page format.

After those experiences, the Macintosh looked like the answer to a prayer. By 1989, we were producing an average of 120 color pages a month—copy, design, production, and mechanicals. Our computers made it possible for three people to do a job that would require a staff of five using conventional means.

We've made a conscious decision to stay as close to the leading edge of desktop publishing technology as the practical applications—putting dots on film for a lithographic press—will allow. By the time this book is published, that will include making four-color continuous-tone separations and merging them with type to create four-color composite film from the desktop.

While that commitment has required a considerable investment of time and money, it has also allowed us to offer clients more services and more convenience. We have gotten clients and projects that we wouldn't have gotten had we not had graphics computers. The income from those projects has far outpaced our investment in technology.

Internally, the move from traditional to digital methods hasn't always been smooth sailing. One designer, after eight months of training, decided that operating a Macintosh design station wasn't her cup of tea. Another balked at doing roughs on the screen. We now make specific Macintosh experience a prerequisite for all staff, full-time and part-time. We will train designers on Quark XPress, our scanners, and our production methods, but their basic knowledge has to include how to operate the Mac and a page layout program.

We've taken pains to be very clear with our printers and clients about our process and the final product. One client, for example, was confused by the laser proofs of page layout files. He thought they were photocopies of the mechanicals and was concerned about the fuzziness of the laser-printed text. When we work with a new printer, we send a sample of our mechanicals (single sheets of repro with crop marks printed on a Linotronic) ahead of the bulk of the job to make sure they're not confused when the materials arrive.

One change that's worth noting is that the computers have made us more selective about the work we take; we now gravitate toward large, complex projects with price tags that justify the investments we have made.

## MARK CRUMPACKER: High Science, Superior Results

*Mark Crumpacker*
*Founded 1989*
*One designer*
*Computer graphics equipment: Macintosh IIcx, Apple Laserwriter IINT, extended keyboard, 105-megabyte hard disk drive, 4 megabytes RAM, 24-bit color scanner, color monitor*

When you picture the freelancer of the future, you have to start with the present. Mark Crumpacker does have one foot firmly planted in the here-and-now, but his steps have taken him far beyond what most studio designers know as safe and acceptable. After starting his career in a large San Francisco agency, he moved out on his own and currently works closely with designer Clement Mok.

Crumpacker still frequently sketches thumbnails on paper. But in his world a "manual" process is one in which the computer has to be explicitly told how and what do, as opposed to one in which it takes directives from the designer and turns them into results. This means adjusting the letterspacing in a page layout by typing in values (such as "110 percent of optimum space maximum") instead of desires (such as "tight but not touching"), for example.

Crumpacker has developed some novel techniques, and by applying them artfully in the right situations, has built a solid client base in the competitive Bay Area market.

The most impressive work Crumpacker does is for large food companies. Using a variety of hardware and software, he creates photo-realistic images of proposed new product packaging with his computer. These new product images are montaged into a "shelf study." When studying a new package, food companies have traditionally made physical mock ups of the most promising designs, then placed them on supermarket shelves stocked with an array of competing products and photographed them. The photos are studied to determine whether the company's packaging can compete in the retail environment.

Crumpacker neatly sidesteps making the comps and taking the photographs by printing the photo-realistic shelf scenes he's built in the computer on a film recorder. This yields 35mm slides for the client to review.

He also works as a design technologist, consulting for Landor Associates and others.

"Studios need an outside consultant to help them keep up with technology," he said. "It's one thing to find out about new products; it's another to find out how they apply to your studio's work. Where people generally go wrong is that they see a new product and decide to buy it without really knowing if it will work in their studio."

The pricetag of a state-of-the-art desktop design station was less than $20,000 just a few years ago. That same equipment could be purchased today for $12,000 or less. But there have been so many new products that a cutting-edge desktop system could now top $60,000 without breaking a sweat. With those kinds of dollars on the line, not to mention your reputation with clients, it makes sense to get the most informed opinion you can.

"It's one thing for vendors and designers to talk about this wonderful technology, but can it be used reliably in a day to day operation? Can people learn it?" Crumpacker said. "One finished product is worth a thousand well-written press releases."

# Chapter Ten:
# The Well-Trained Studio

**Up The Learning Curve**

**Training Aids: SIGs, Help Lines, And Videotapes**

## Up The Learning Curve

Learning to use a graphics computer is like most things in life; it's a little harder than chewing gum, but it's not brain surgery, either. If you get a little outside help and make a mental commitment to becoming a digital designer, you can be producing camera-ready mechanicals on the screen in a few weeks..

The learning curve is steepest for PostScript illustration programs such as FreeHand® and Illustrator®. While the basic steps—tracing a template, changing line weights and sizes, scaling, skewing, and filling—can be understood quickly, many designers say it takes several months of daily use to learn the fine points of the programs. It's not that these programs are terribly difficult to learn; it's just that there are so many possibilities, so many tools, that it takes a while for your mind to grasp them all. Editing Bezier curves is tricky. Until you get accustomed to working with a mouse and screen instead of a pencil and paper, you may feel clumsy, like you're trying to dissect a carburetor with a tire iron. For designers used to feeling a well-practiced harmony with their tools, that can be frustrating.

By contrast, a good working knowledge of most page layout programs, fonts, word processors, and PostScript laser printers can be developed in a few weeks.

Scanning and imaging software are relatively simple, too, though it may take some fiddling to settle into a procedure that's effective and find the scanner settings that work best.

Once you've mastered two or three core programs, the others will come much easier as the basic commands are pretty consistent from program to program.

### Can I Really Teach Myself?

We've heard dozens of designers say that they've never had to read a manual to learn Macintosh software. Several of our manuals are well-thumbed, but the majority are used as reference guides, consulted only in a crisis. It's also true, however, that many of the designers who "never read a manual" watched someone use the programs first.

The designers we interviewed all agreed on one point: Using a graphics computer for design isn't a skill you can learn from a book. They also say it's hard to learn in a classroom. Without exception, they say the best way to learn is to use the computer on real projects. That way, you'll quickly home in on the techniques that fit you and your work best. You *can* do this on your own. But there's an initial stage where everything takes twice as long and seems twice as complicated as it should. The length of this awkward stage varies, but invariably, designers say you can get through it more quickly by hiring an outside trainer to show you the way.

### The Outside Advantage

Learning to use a graphics computer involves a lot of different abilities: Motor skills, hand-eye-coordination, some left-brain logic, memorization. How did you learn to drive a car? Someone took you out on the road and showed you, right? Same thing with a graphics computer. Having someone there to give you feedback and clues while you work at the computer makes you learn better and learn faster.

"We've been to a few workshops, but sitting in a room listening to someone describe how to use the software didn't help us much," said Pat Davis, a Sacramento designer whose studio operates five Macintosh workstations. "Instead of taking courses, I have a freelance designer who knows the system really well on call. If someone in the studio needs help with a technique or has a problem on a project, the trainer comes in, sits with the designer, and helps them work it through. If someone shows you how to apply a technique to your own work, you remember it better than if you saw them demonstrate it on a hypothetical project."

Davis said the freelance trainer charges $40 per hour.

Illustrator Lance Hidy recalls that, when he first began using Adobe's Illustrator software, he was buffaloed by its complexity. The solution was simple: "A friend who knows Illustrator came over. In two hours, he taught me the basics. Once I had those, I taught myself."

Full-time staff members train the designers at Landor Associates in San Francisco. These staff members sit with the designers as they design, improving their skills using actual projects as the lesson material. Hans Flink, the New York-based package designer, has a trainer come in once a week to work with his associates one on one .

Some studios hire designers with computer knowledge specifically to get their graphics computers working and train their designers. Bryan O'Neill was enticed to leave his freelance practice to play this role at Hornall Anderson Design Works in Seattle. O'Neill has been successful, taking the studio to the point where 75 percent of the firm's jobs go through a Macintosh at some point.

Other studios use the "diffusion" model for training. One designer is given a graphics computer and encouraged to figure out how it works. As he learns, he begins showing the others how the system works. That's how Mark Crumpacker started his career in a large San Francisco studio.

"I was an intern at the time, so they could give me a computer without worrying that projects were going to be delayed while I learned," Crumpacker said. Eventually, Crumpacker did learn the system and began teaching the others. With his help, most were able to pick it up.

There are exceptions: "Not everyone is cut out to operate a graphics computer. We had one person who couldn't master it. He worked at it

hard enough, but for months, nothing happened," Crumpacker explained. "They're rare, but there *are* people who just don't get it. I have no idea why, but they don't."

An argument in favor of having at least one semi-portable Macintosh (a Plus, SE, or SE/30) in the studio is for training. Some studios encourage designers to take a machine home and play with it after work.

## Playtime Is The Best Time

One of the best ways to increase your skills in any program is to play "find the features." There are two approaches to this, the logical and the serendipitous. Pick whichever suits you best. The logical approach is to park yourself in front of the computer. While reading the software manual, try out each of the program's features. Not all of it will stick, of course, but even experienced users will find one or two goodies they didn't know about. The unstructured approach is to simply open the program and diddle with it. Try opening all the menus and activating each menu item in turn.

## On Those Days When It All Goes Wrong

Some years ago, a journalist came across this bit of graffiti on a restroom wall in the computer science building at the Massachusetts Institute of Technology: "How come you never do what I want, only what I tell you?"

There are going to be times when you're convinced that the machine takes a fiendish delight in thwarting your every request. While there are mysterious maladies that strike without warning, especially in the first six months, it's more likely that you're just not being clear with the computer about what it is that you desire. Forget the fact that the software manual is written in a way that would take a team of CIA cipher experts a decade to decode. Don't be shy; if you get stumped, call everyone you even vaguely suspect might be able to help you. The first place we always start is with the manufacturer. We don't know the technical support people and we won't have to run into them dropping off type at the service bureau. It's amazing how much some vendors *don't* know about their products. Occasionally, you'll find a reference to a technique in the software manual that just won't work. Often enough, these turn out to be features that were never activated in the software. A quick call to technical support can save you a lot of frustration. Some developers charge an annual fee for access to their technical support. For complex programs or ones you use frequently, seriously consider paying the support fee.

*Users groups:* If you're new to graphics computers, a users group should be part of your support network. You'll have to invest some time. Most users groups meet for two to three hours a month. Many colleges have very strong users groups. While the group members might be more rabid about computers than you are, if you need information, this is a ready-made pool of experience that costs very little to access. (See *Refernce And Resources*, page 151, for information on finding a users group.)

*Service bureaus:* An even easier way to find experienced users is at your service bureau. These folks use the gear every day. Since you're doing business with them, most are happy to share tips and techniques. Some service bureaus also offer training (see *Graphic Connexions,* page 130).

*Communications services:* Computer information services, such as GEnie and CompuServe, can be helpful. Using a modem and telephone line, you connect your computer to the service's computer. Once connected, you'll be able to explore "message areas" within the service, called Special Interest Groups (SIGs).

Experienced users "talk" to each other by leaving messages in the SIG message area. CompuServe has SIGs devoted to desktop publishing, graphics and illustration, and to specific software companies.

Aside from computer talk, you'll be able to review and copy software programs. You can download screen fonts (the characters the computer uses to display text on the monitor) from the Adobe forum on CompuServe. There are volumes of digitized images and clip-art available, too.

*Books:* There are books covering most major software packages, such as Quark XPress, PageMaker, and Illustrator. These are generally much easier to understand than the software manuals. It's worth $30 apiece to have books that will help you master your core programs. The books are also valuable reference tools.

*Periodicals:* The most useful publication we've found is *Step-By-Step Electronic Design* published by Dynamic Graphics. This newsletter covers one or two graphics techniques in great detail each month, showing how a computer was used to create a specific effect or project.

*Videotapes:* You've seen the *Jane Fonda Workout* tape; are you ready for the *Famous Art Directors Digital Wash and Gouache*? Instructional videotapes are available that cover many of the major graphics programs. Tapes are useful because they show the techniques in action, which printed manuals can't. We found the introductory tape produced by Adobe about Illustrator quite helpful. It explained the basic elements of the program succinctly and demonstrated the use of each of the program's tools.

All of these resources cam help you in your quest for technical nirvana, but there's no substitute for sitting at the computer punching keys until you get it right. Don't go it alone, however. Get some outside help; and if all else fails, read the instructions.

# Chapter Eleven:
# Working With A Service Bureau

**Pick Your Partners—Carefully**

**Test Your Service Bureau**

**You've Got A Friend:  Upgrading Services**

They used to be called typesetters, or with a little more flourish, composing houses. Since the advent of desktop publishing, businesses that set type—convert disk files from graphics computers to reproduction quality type—call themselves "service bureaus." Some are, and some aren't.

If you produce mechanical art or film for your clients, there may be no link that's more important—or over which you have as little control—as the service bureau. A good one can be your best friend; a lackadaisical one can be your worst nightmare.

Not all service bureaus are created equal. There are plenty of places, from quick printers to pre-press shops, that have imagesetters and a graphics computer. They can print your files. They may or may not do it well. You'll never know *how* well until you work with them.

### Evening Up The Odds

Three ways to increase the odds of having a good experience are to interview, check references, and have the bureau print test files. Ask other designers who have graphics computers about service bureaus. You can also get references from Linotronic and Agfa Compugraphic, manufacturers of two of the most popular imagesetters. (Telephone numbers for Linotronic and Agfa Compugraphic are listed in *Reference And Resources*, page 151.) Ask for the name of the manufacturers' sales manager for your area. Call and ask the sales manager to recommend the two or three bureaus he feels are most aggressively serving design studios.

Interview the service bureaus. Ask for references from other local designers and talk to them about the bureau's service: Do they meet their scheduled delivery times? How knowledgeable are they about graphics computers? What specific programs does the service bureau print

files from? Have there been any unexpected problems? How were they resolved? Ask how many imagesetters they have. Two imagesetters are better than one; there's less chance your jobs will get bumped off the imagesetter by another customer's rush work, or that delivery of graphics-intensive files (which can take half an hour or more per page to print) will be delayed.

When you've narrowed your choices to two or three shops, visit them. Talk to the production manager one-on-one. Show them the type of work you do. Talk about the software programs you're using now and those you plan to work with over the next six months. Find out whether there are people at the service bureau who have the skills and—most important—the experience to help you work through the process of learning to prepare files so that the results are what you expected. Sure, you thought that an electronic file, once finished, is cut-and-dried; that there isn't much room for interpretation on the part of the service bureau. That *is* your goal. However, as Shakespeare noted, there's many a slip 'twixt lip and cup. Some of the more common slips include:

*Font conflicts:* Font conflicts—in which an imagesetter refuses to recognize or substitutes fonts—have been a problem with desktop publishing since the first connection between the Macintosh and high-resolution imagesetters.

Service bureaus say font conflicts are still a common occurrence, especially with clients who are new to graphics computers. Designers confirm that they sometimes receive repro from a service bureau that's not set in the fonts specified in their files.

In this case, the Macintosh is a victim of its own success. Both the computer and the imagesetter identify fonts by number, rather than by name. Back in 1984, no one suspected that the Macintosh would revolutionize the graphic arts—or that the bulk of the typefaces available for traditional photocomposers would one day be converted for use on the Macintosh. Apple didn't reserve enough numbers in the Macintosh operating system (only 255) to assign a unique number to each of the hundreds of fonts that have been released since.

Also, there is no clearing house for font numbers; each font manufacturer is free to pick among the 255 available numbers as they choose. It would probably be easier to live with this situation if the conflicts were confined to seldom-used display faces. They aren't; even common text faces carry duplicate numbers.

Thus, the conflict. Your computer shows a headline as Times Roman; the imagesetter, reading the number, sees it as Janson Text. The problem is especially acute when designers mix Adobe fonts with fonts from other manufacturers. Most service bureaus use the Adobe font library as their core of faces. They're used to preventing conflicts between Adobe faces. When you throw in that radical font you bought from the Ring People Of Saturn Software Company, you increase the odds of a conflict.

The NFNT numbering system released in 1989 has helped. Ask your bureau if they've converted to the NFNT system. Some service bureaus supply a complete set of NFNT screen fonts on disk for a small charge. Using the bureau's screen fonts to create your documents will help if you're having conflict problems.

So does the use of a font utility such as Suitcase II® or Master Juggler®. These programs segregate fonts into separate "suitcases" to keep them from conflicting with each other.

You have to do your part, too, by clearly identifying to the service bureau which fonts are in your file. Use a transmittal form, such as the one on the following page.

One way to avoid font conflicts and other errors in page layout files is to save them as a straight PostScript file instead of saving them in the page layout program's "native" data format. PageMaker®, Quark XPress®, and other programs allow you to do this. Rather than re-opening the PostScript file in the program in which it was created (and possibly introducing font conflicts), the service bureau sends the PostScript file directly to the imagesetter. One fly in the ointment is that, while PageMaker files decrease in size when you save them as straight PostScript, files from some other programs (Xpress, for one) balloon—growing to three or four times their original size.

*PostScript errors:* PostScript is a wonderful page description language, but it's not without faults. One of them is that its imaging method takes enormous amounts of RAM. The higher the resolution of the printer, the more RAM is needed. It takes more space to remember where to put enough dots to fill a page at 1270 dpi resolution than it does at 300 dpi because there are so many more dots.

When a PostScript printer runs out of RAM, it issues a terse "PostScript Error" message to the computer. There's usually nothing physically wrong with the file, but it won't print. Ironically, some files that print fine on your 300 dpi laser printer will positively choke an imagesetter, particularly one with an early-model RIP (Raster Image Processor). The RIP is the interface that translates PostScript commands from your file into control codes that tell the imagesetter where to put the dots.

Linotronic has released three RIPs to date. RIP 1 sometimes chokes on complex page layouts. RIP 2 will image most page layout files, as long as you don't have too many large PostScript illustrations in them. RIP 3 does a good job with even very large PostScript illustration files. Linotronic has announced a new model, RIP 4, which will supposedly increase printing speed for color separations and other complex documents. Ask which RIP your ser-

---

### FORM ENSURES FUNCTION: Use A Transmittal When You Send Files To Type

Getting repro that matches what you thought you sent the service bureau is your responsibility, too. If your service bureau has a transmittal form, use it—or create your own. The critical information is the name of the files, number of pages, and what fonts and programs were used.

---

**BLOUNT + WALKER VISUAL COMMUNICATIONS, INC.**     *PostScript Service Order*

Date Entered: _____      Page Size: _____
Date Due: _____      ❑ with crops      ❑ without crops
Our PO #: _____      ❑ paper positive      ❑ paper negative
Total Pages: _____      ❑ film positive      ❑ film negative
❑ color seps      ❑ other

| File Name | Pages | Program(s) | Graphics | Fonts |
|---|---|---|---|---|
| CDBP/Chap 1 | 6 | XPress, Cricket Graph | ✓ | Times Roman, Helv Bold, Helv Cond, Zapf Dingb |
| CDBP/Chap 2 | 16 | XPress, Cricket Graph | ✓ | Times Roman, Helv Bold, Helv Cond, Zapf Dingb |
| CDBP/Chap 3 | 8 | XPress | | Times Roman, Helv Bold, Helv Cond, Zapf Dingb |
| CDBP/Chap 4 | 10 | Xpress, Cricket Graph | ✓ | Times Roman, Helv Bold, Helv Cond, Zapf Dingb |
| CDBP/Chap 5 | 8 | XPress | | Times Roman, Helv Bold, Helv Cond, Zapf Dingb |
| CDBP/Chap 6 | 6 | XPress | | Times Roman, Helv Bold, Helv Cond, Zapf Dingb |
| CDBP/Chap 7 | 18 | XPress | | Times Roman, Helv Bold, Helv Cond, Zapf Dingb |
| CDBP/Chap 8 | 4 | XPress | | Times Roman, Helv Bold, Helv Cond, Zapf Dingb |

If there are questions about these files, please call: Blount + Walker Visual Communications / VOICE: 001-555-0000 / FAX: 001-555-0000

---

vice bureau has. The RIP 2 is adequate for most files, but if you plan to run film separations from Illustrator® or FreeHand® files, look for a shop with a RIP 3.

***Test, test, test:*** Given the early stage of graphics computer technology and the wide variety of software available, it's unreasonable for you to walk into a service bureau and expect them to own and expertly operate every program. The test of a good service bureau is not whether they know *everything*—none of them do—but whether they can find out what they *need* to know to do a good job for you.

Take in test files that are typical of your work; files created using the packages you use most frequently. Before beginning a relationship with a service bureau, have them set these test files. If there are problems, work with the bureau to iron them out.

***Ask about the bureau's tests:*** Conscientious bureaus test their processing chemicals, paper, film, and imagesetters on a regular basis to catch and correct any inconsistencies. The formulation of the paper and chemicals they buy can vary slightly from batch to batch. A screen set at 50 percent on one batch of paper might be lighter or darker than one set on a different batch. If you're working on a project over several weeks, it's important to get type densities that match from page to page.

*Perform your own tests:* Most imagesetters in use today were designed to produce type—not line screens, halftones, or color separations. If you will use any of these, ask your service bureau to provide you with test strips that show the actual screen densities they're producing from the program(s) you use. At a minimum, you'll need screens ranging from zero percent black to 100 percent black in 10 percent increments. One percent increments would be better. Ask the bureau to check the steps with a densitometer and write the readings underneath. You may find that the steps are unequal; the density may increase more from 50 percent to 60 percent than it does from 60 percent to 70 percent.

Producing quality color separations on equipment designed for black and white work is tricky. There are wide variations between what you see on a color monitor and what you'll get on the film. If you're simulating Pantone colors using tints of process colors, look out. No two programs mix the tints the same way for Pantone colors. The PMS 469 in a Freehand® illustration may not match the PMS 469 specified in XPress for a headline.

For color-critical work, this can be a problem. San Francisco designer Mark Crumpacker is a consultant to Landor Associates and designs packaging for large consumer products companies. For product labels, the color match has to be exact. Crumpacker calibrated his computer and software by creating a file containing swatches of all the Pantone colors. He sent the file to his service bureau and had it set as separation film. The service bureau made a set of colors keys from the separations. Now, Crumpacker has a complete swatch book. He uses the color key swatches, not his computer monitor, to judge colors.

Another solution is to find a service bureau with an Iris or 4Cast printer. These are proofing devices that can make four-color process proofs directly from electronic files. Dale Glasgow, an illustrator based in Arlington, Virginia, uses the 4Cast to provide clients with proofs of Freehand illustrations and has found it to be extremely accurate. The 4Cast is made by DuPont. Their sales office ( see *Reference And Resources*, page 151) can give you the name of the nearest facility that has a 4Cast. Color accuracy is the next frontier for graphics computers. New products, such as attachments that calibrate color monitors and new kinds of color printers will probably ameliorate this problem over the next few years.

*Send a laser print:* Always include a laser print of your files when sending them for output. The service bureau can print your file on their laser prior to printing it on an imagesetter and compare their laser proof to yours. If there are any discrepancies, they can fix them or call you. If you send files to the bureau via modem, fax a transmittal form and a laser print.

## Buddy Up For Safety

A good service bureau will be a partner, not just a vendor. More than equipment and lab tests, the people make the difference. Hire for attitude; people who care about getting your job right are the people who *will* get your job right. Mark Crumpacker said he does business with one or two production managers, and he follows them when they move from service bureau to service bureau. In bureau-rich San Francisco, that's an option. Your options may be more limited.

Service bureaus that are heavily committed to desktop technology tend to keep up with the latest hardware and software products. The most active bureaus are beta-test sites for the products. They can be an excellent source of information on equipment and techniques. Share your experiences with the bureau and they'll probably reciprocate. Be a friend, not just a customer. You'll get loads of free advice, most of it good.

## GRAPHIC CONNEXIONS: Service, And Then Some

"Anybody can set files for customers. We're trying to add value to the output by being a knowledge resource for our clients," said Derek White, president of Graphic Connexions, a Cranbury, New Jersey, service bureau. "We have experience with a lot of different software and hardware. We can help designers when they run into problems. Sometimes we can help them find a way to use existing products to create a new solution that meets some need they have."

The company has deep roots in both traditional pre-press processes and the latest desktop technology. Its parent firm is Market-Source, a company that creates marketing programs for consumer products companies. Graphic Connexions began as an in-house front end for MarketSource's press operation. White, the former marketing director for a large computer supplier in northern New Jersey, was brought in to turn the in-house typesetting department into a service bureau. His approach? He added service. Lots of it.

"Graphics computers have brought a lot of people into the production process who aren't familiar with the technical details of getting high-quality results," White said. "This is less true of designers than of corporate clients. Still, designers aren't *supposed* to know how to make screen densities match precisely on a Linotronic 300. Many of them don't *want* to know. We can make it happen for them.

"When we tested Illustrator, we found that film densities for screens can vary as much as 20 percent from what's specified in the file. We have a PostScript programmer who wrote patches for the printer driver files to give us accurate densities. If a client's specifies a 50 percent tint, they get a 50 percent tint.

"A good service bureau will take the time to calibrate their equipment. They also need to be good detectives, able to track down and solve the small problems that crop up when printing complex files or files from new software programs."

Like some other service bureaus, Graphic Connexions tries to make a variety of services available with a maximum of convenience. A twenty-four hour bulletin board accepts files via modem. Clients can choose one of three service levels: one-day turnaround, six hours, or while-you-wait. A twenty-four bit color scanner and color laser printer are on hand for color design and output. Staff designers can help with or even create PostScript illustrations, video animation, three-dimensional graphics, and hypermedia presentations. A link between Graphic Connexions and a nearby Scitex installation gives clients the option of working with desktop color equipment for design and comps, then sending the files to a Scitex Visionary system. Photos are scanned and the composite film is output using the ultra-high quality Scitex equipment.

Helping customers learn how to use these new processes successfully isn't just good marketing, it's also a good service in itself.

"We run a bureau orientation for clients. They bring their employees and we show them how we work—how we can work *with* them to get the best results," White said. "The technology for creating and reproducing quality artwork—even four-color process separations—on desktop computers is available, but the knowledge of how to use it isn't widespread. We see ourselves helping clients by helping them apply the technology they've bought to solving problems."

# Chapter Twelve:
# Managing A Computer System

*Keeping It All Together—And Working*

*Software Compatibility And Power Solutions*

*Well-Furnished Workstations: Are Ergonomics Necessary?*

While they are designed to run with little maintenance, installing and maintaining a graphics computer system does take some effort.

There are two immediate questions to answer: Will you install more than four machines? And if so, will they be tied together in a network?

The number of computer stations has a direct bearing on how much time you'll spend keeping all of the loose ends—software updates, cleaning disks, checking cables—from unraveling. Even with two or three computers, someone in the studio will have to take on the role of chief technologist. It can be you, it can be someone who already works with you, you can hire someone to come in from the outside (see *Hornall Anderson*, page 116), or you can have a consultant help (see *Mark Crumpacker*, page 120, and *Outside Advantage*, page 122).

Many designers find that, once they've researched the equipment before making a purchase and have begun working on a graphics computer, they become fascinated by the technology—or at least interested enough to want to keep up with it.

However you handle the role of designer/technologist is up to you; but to get the most from your system creatively and economically, you need to get it handled.

## Big Systems Keep On Rolling

In the world of IBM PC networks, ten users in one office amount to no more than an amoeba in an elephant's intestine. In the world of graphics computers, an installation of ten or more workstations is big; big enough to require a full-time administrator.

The administrator should be someone with a keen interest in the technology, who has an affinity for machines and is adept at deductive and inductive reasoning. They should also have a high threshold of frustration—because there's going to be some. If you manage to contract a virus (see page 139) or get some buggy software, the frustration factor can skyrocket.

The administrator of a large system should read the major computer publications each month and plan on attending at least one trade fair each year. As the point man, designated question-answerer, and fix-it person, a lot of the administrator's time will be taken up helping other designers use the system better.

All Macintosh computers come with a built-in network capability. They can be connected to an AppleTalk network using the existing printer port—in fact they have to be to access a PostScript printer. As supplied by Apple, AppleTalk does little except send files to the printer. With additional software, such as TOPS®, InBox®, or Timbuktu®, it can be upgraded to a functional link capable of transferring files from station to station, supporting electronic mail, spooling print files, central storage of your fonts to free disk space on the individual workstations, and more. Some of these arrangements require dedicating one computer as a file server. A file server is a central filing cabinet and traffic cop, directing electronic traffic on the network, spooling files to be printed, and sending files shared by several designers back and forth. Today, most design studios still use the reliable "sneaker net" system: When designers need to transfer a file to someone, they put it on a floppy and walk it across the room.

"A very basic network is enough for a studio where everyone can see each other," said Mark Crumpacker. "It's nice to have a full-function network if you're moving big files around from machine to machine, but you need a very fast network, such as Ethernet."

Ethernet is a hardware/communications standard for networking computers. Using an add-in circuit card and special wiring, it allows computers to send files at speeds many times that of AppleTalk.

If you plan to get into color, however, even that may not be enough.

At *MacWeek*, designers separate and strip the entire publication on a Macintosh system. The size of the color files—which range up to 4 mb—chokes the network, slowing all other traffic to a crawl. For transferring these files, *MacWeek* relies on sneaker net, trading data on removable 45 mb cartridges.

If you decide you must have a network, hire someone who is experienced with Macintosh data networks to recommend and install the network for you.

## Clean Machines

You sweep the crumbs out of your toaster, right? Well, someone needs to keep the dust bunnies out of the design computers. The first level of maintenance involves removing dust and other foreign objects (paper clips, eraser dust, shreds of paper) from the CPU, the keyboard, and the area surrounding them.

In small studios, everyone can be responsible for their own Mac, but only if they've been briefed on the basics: don't use solvents anywhere near a computer; don't touch the pins of a SCSI device or the SCSI port to avoid frying the computer's chips with static electricity; the power to the computer should be shut off before a SCSI device is unplugged or plugged in; use a specially designed vacuum to suck the dust out of the computer rather than blowing it with a rubber syringe or your breath; and clean the heads of your floppy disk once a month with a commercial disk cleaner (available at computer supply stores).

It's important that anyone who works with a computer think about the safety of the machine. In one service bureau, a designer was having trouble with his mouse. He decided that the metal plug that connects the mouse to the computer needed to be cleaned. He sprayed it with electrical contact cleaner and plugged it back in. Since it was still wet, it blew the computer's logic board ($800-plus). The designer figured something had gone wrong with the computer, but, still curious as to whether the mouse worked, he plugged it into (and blew up) yet another computer before a co-worker stopped him. Using common sense will prevent most incidents of this kind.

## Back It Up

One of the most important—and onerous—maintenance tasks is backing up data files. Data can and does disappear for no apparent reason. Files mysteriously refuse to open, or they open, but contain no information.

The only truly elegant solution for maintaining backups is to have a tape drive or large optical disk connected to a network file server. The server can automatically poll and back up the data from each machine every day. Even if you already have a file server, adding a tape or optical drive and automatic backup software can cost $1,500 to $4,500 (see page 39 for more information on optical disk and cartridge drives).

The next-best alternative is to have each designer make copies of project files on floppy disks daily. Then, once a week, someone can go from machine to machine with a 45 mb removable cartridge drive and backup all the data on the drive onto a cartridge. The drives can be bought for less than $1,000 and the cartridges cost about $75 each. The first time a hard disk crashes just before a deadline, you'll recover every cent of that and more. The cartridges have become a standard in the graphic arts industry and are used extensively by publishers, service bureaus, and illustrators to transfer large files.

# Software Compatibility And Power Solutions

### Software Compatibility

Having different versions of software and data files on a network can be troubling. Even having multiple versions on machines that aren't networked can create unnecessary frustration.

If you have more than one machine, you should be sure that the software matches from computer to computer. If one designer installs an upgrade of a program, then gives the file to another designer using an older version, there's a good chance it won't open or print properly. Because of the problems with font conflicts (see page 126), even having different fonts or having the same fonts in a different configuration can lead to difficulties.

When you install your initial software, make sure you install the same programs in the same way on each machine. Generally, following the recommendations in the developer's manual works well. We strongly recommend the use of a font management utility (see page 103). Take the time to make one standard arrangement of the fonts, then install it on each machine.

Most organizations that have a number of desktop computers do not allow anyone to bring in software and copy it to their machines. Aside from the legal question of the license for that software, uncontrolled disk-swapping is a prime cause of virus infections. Just don't allow it.

Standardizing data files is a bit more difficult but, if anything, more important. Computers allow you to store data in a number of different ways, according to what suits your mood. With the Macintosh, for example, you can keep data files loose on your "desktop," or you can place them in folders or volumes, or even partition off pieces of the hard disk for specific purposes.

One thing that makes designers creative is a sense of individuality, a desire to do things their own way. But when it comes to storing data, individuality is bad. The reason is simple. Just as your financial files are most useful and least likely to get lost if you keep them organized in a filing cabinet by account number and name, data files are easiest to keep track of if you organize them in a folder that has been named in a way that others in the studio can quickly find and identify. If you're not available when a file is needed —you're away from the office or a meteorite has fallen on you—someone can pick up your work and carry on.

Although the Macintosh allows a lot of freedom in naming files created on it, for project files, we follow a specific format. We agree on a "slug" for the project, usually the client's name or an abbreviation of the title of the project: CDBP/2, for example, is the name of the file for chapter two of this book. It's critical to keep track of files going to and coming from the service bureau also. Multiple chapters, pages, or elements from several projects may go to the service bureau at the same time, so keep them tagged. We use a date, project identifier, sequential batch identifier, and number of pages as our code: 2.14 CDBP/A-24 is the first file sent to the service bureau for this book. It's twenty-four pages long and was transmitted on Valentine's Day. This file would be kept on the hard disk, in a folder named CDBP Type Final, which would be contained in a folder named CDBP. This may seem overly rigid, but when your hard disk contains over a thousand individual files, organization is essential. If someone needs a file on a hard disk, they shouldn't have to hunt through folders named "new work" or "Jay's files" or "what is this, anyway?" It also makes it easy to locate files using a file finder utility. These handy little programs can search your hard disk for a file, then show you where it's located. You can't search for a file if you don't know what you might have named it. In this case, we could search for the type file by asking the file finder to look for all files named CDBP, all files named 2.14, all files that had a suffix of 24, or that were a "Batch A." This kind of system also makes it easier for your service bureau to track and report back to you on the status of your work.

As a starting point, you might want to create separate folders for each one of your major clients and keep information relating to those clients—correspondence, estimates, requests, project files—in individual folders inside that folder. This system is really no different from the "job jacket" system used successfully by printers for years.

Keep working files and final files ready to go to the service bureau clearly marked and separated. The first time you send a draft file to the service bureau instead of a final file, it may not cost you too much. Done consistently, this will jack up your type bills and play havoc with your deadlines.

## Making Your New Friend Comfortable

The physical environment your computer system inhabits is important, too. Most desktop computers are happiest in a clean, air-conditioned space, but will operate in temperatures up to 100°F as long as the humidity in the air doesn't condense on their internal parts. The Macintosh Plus was not provided with an internal fan, so it tends to suffer most in intense heat.

*Siting:* Don't put computers in direct sunlight or in walking paths. Place them in a spot where they can breathe and where the air vents on the top, sides, and bottom aren't covered or obstructed.

*Clean power:* "Clean" power is electricity that is free of radio and electromagnetic interference and that is at a constant voltage close to 120 volts a.c. Most people are aware that power surges, sudden spikes or peaks in the current, can destroy the chips inside the CPU. A good surge protector (not a cheap, department-store model) will keep most of these from getting through and will filter out "noise" in the current caused by interference from other equipment, such as a copier. We've used the "power director" model sold by Radio Shack for several years with good results. One of them took a blast from a lightning bolt that struck a power line outside our studio. The surge fried the protector, but the computer was unharmed.

Voltage drops can be as harmful to a computer as power surges. It's very common for the voltage coming into your office to rise and fall, with the current dipping below 120 volts frequently. A friend who operated a computer-driven advertising display board in downtown San Francisco was shocked to learn that the power there is purposely cut for hours on end. After several chips blew in quick succession, he called the power company. They told him they let the voltage drop to 90 volts most evenings after dark. Running a computer on low voltage for extended periods can destroy its power supply, the monitor, and other vital organs. If the lights in your office flicker frequently, you're probably having voltage drops. Buy an Uninterruptible Power Supply. This is a unit that takes electricity from a wall socket, stores it briefly, and then doles it out to your computer at a perfectly steady 120 volts. If the wall socket should go dead during a power outage, the UPS can keep your computer running long enough to save the file you're working on and shut the system down so that the hard disk and data files aren't damaged. UPS units aren't cheap; one big enough to run a black and white design station costs between $500 and $1,000.

Your best bet is to have an electrician install at least one circuit that is completely isolated from all other equipment in your office. This will prevent the computer from being slapped around when the water cooler starts up or the air conditioning unit kicks in. If you can't get a clean circuit, at least get a UPS.

# Well-Furnished Workstations: Are Ergonmics Necessary?

Computers of all types have produced a huge windfall for the makers of office furniture. "Ergonomically" engineered chairs, desks, lamps, and work surfaces have been joined by anti-static mats, glare filters, and even motor-operated copy holders. It may sound like a boondoggle— and the pricing on some of these items lends credibility to that suspicion— but special desks, chairs, and filters do address a very serious problem. As office workers have switched from typewriters and telephones to terminals and headsets, the number of people complaining of headaches, fatigue, wrist aches, neck problems, even nausea, has grown tremendously. The furniture makers have tried to create furnishing that will help make you and your equipment as comfortable as possible while reducing the risk of injury.

Very little of this new furniture is in use in design studios. Surprisingly, few designers report the kind of low-intensity, chronic pain that ordinary office workers complain of. Maybe we've gotten used to being uncomfortable after all those years leaning over a drafting board.

There are some designers, however, who say their necks and shoulders, in particular, hurt after a long day in front of the computer. Mousing is not an ergonomically sound activity; if you have weak wrists it can become painful in just a short time. Eyestrain is also a common complaint among designers.

## Furniture Grade

The custom computer furniture sold by Foster, Anthro, and others can help. The object of their furniture is to organize the computer hardware so that it's accessible and positioned properly, and to give you enough working space to take care of your other tasks. Several studios, including Hornall Anderson Design Works and Pat Davis Design, have had custom furniture built for their designers.

Most of these configurations are U-shaped. The computer hardware is kept to one side of the unit, with cables running in special inset channels to keep them off the floor. A drawing board occupies the other side of the U, with drawer space below, upper shelves for software manuals and reference guides above, and sometimes overhead cabinets.

The work surfaces used for computers should be adjustable, so they can be raised and lowered like a drafting table. This will accommodate people of different heights, and the height can be changed to suit a specific task. The computer monitor should be tilted up or raised off the desk so that you don't have to crane your neck down or hunch your shoulders to see the screen. Monitor platforms that attach to the work table and allow you to "float" the monitor anywhere over the work surface are the best answer. The floats costs between $90 and $300. Also, you can buy units that hold a Macintosh SE or Plus on a special platform that can be tilted up for easier viewing.

An adjustable chair is essential. Some designers report they work well in a secretarial-style chair with a pneumatic lift. Others say that a chair with padded arms can help keep your shoulders from being strained when typing or mousing. One designer we know prefers an executive-style recliner, complete with fold-out footrest. He says that reclining in the chair takes pressure off of his lower back. Placing a pillow in the small of your back can also keep you from hunching forward—a prime cause of back pain.

Designers tend to focus on the monitor too intensely. They don't blink as often as they otherwise would, and they don't move their muscles. To help prevent injury, as you work, look away from the monitor frequently. Remember to blink. Shift your focus from the keyboard, to the monitor, and back. Get up and shake out your muscles *at least* once an hour. Flex your legs in between these stretches. If you don't consciously minimize the effects of sitting at a terminal all day, the cost of your computer system in dollars may pale in comparison with the pain you suffer from chronic injuries.

# Chapter Thirteen: Things That Can—And Will—Go Wrong

**Common Problems: A Few Of Our Least Favorite Things**

**Viral Infections: Causes, Cures**

Graphics computers are, of course, a mixed blessing. Most of the time, you'll agree with Marc Passarelli (*Tale Of Two Studios*, page 14): "Thank God I bought a Mac." There will also be times when you'll swear you'd rather go spearfishing naked with sharks than wrestle with that damned box again. These occasions will be marked by extreme frustration; usually frustration at the realization there's a very simple explanation for the problem that's bedeviling you. Some problems can't be prevented. If a logic board is going to evaporate in a puff of smoke, there's not much you can do about it except buy a backup machine so the studio's work doesn't grind to a halt while the computer's being fixed. If a hard disk is going to crash, it's going to crash. Your role is to make backup copies of your data at the end of each day and hope you never need them.

Some of the expectable problems can be prevented, though.

### Who's On First?

Despite the homogeneity of the world Apple created for the Macintosh, there's still some potential for incompatibility. Incompatibility is a fancy way of saying that the whoosis won't talk to the whatsis. The potential causes are legion, but the most common are:

*Bad cabling:* The Macintosh uses a communications port, called a SCSI (Small Computer System Interface) to talk to peripherals such as external hard disks and some scanners. The SCSI is very fast, transferring data quickly. It's also very finicky, as the total length of the cables connected to a SCSI port must fall within a certain range, and there have to be resistors (called terminators) at certain points in the SCSI wiring. SCSI termination is more of an art than a science. If your computer is otherwise normal but won't recognize an external hard disk, scanner,

or other SCSI device, suspect the wiring. Check all the connectors, snugging them up tightly. Try changing the cables, the length of the cables, or the order in which different devices are plugged into the SCSI circuit. Also, all SCSI devices connected to a Macintosh have to be turned *on* in order for the computer to boot. If you have SCSI devices and can't boot your computer, make sure the SCSI devices have power going to them and that they are on. A dealer can be very helpful in solving SCSI problems.

*System files:* You may also have a bad system file. The system file is the first thing the computer looks at when you turn it on. If the system file is damaged, if you have more than one copy of the system file anywhere on your hard disk, or if you have other software that's conflicting with the system file, your computer may not even "boot," remaining dormant and refusing to come on at all.

It will also do this when the logic board fails. To find out if the computer is working at all, try starting it from the internal floppy drive by booting from a floppy you know has a working system file on it.

Apple allows various small programs, called INITs and CDEVs, to be installed directly into the system file each time the machine is turned on. Not all of them are compatible. A conflict between two INITs will cause the machine to hang up during the boot process. If your computer won't boot from its hard drive, start it up with a floppy disk, open the hard drive, and take all the INITs and CDEVs out of the system folder. Then restart. If it boots, one of the INITs was the problem. Replace them in the system folder one by one, restarting after each addition until you find which one caused the problem.

Troubleshooting SCSI and system problems is covered in the instruction manuals that come with the equipment. Read the sections of the manuals dealing with the initial set-up of the computer and its hard disk drive carefully. If they begin misbehaving, try re-reading the manual. Don't keep performing the same tests over and over, however. If you go through the steps outlined in the manual and still can't get the computer to run, call the dealer you bought the equipment from.

*File compatibility:* If your computer boots and runs properly, but you can't transfer data files between programs smoothly, there is some incompatibility at work. Illustrations and scanned art are especially prone to this kind of behavior. There are several standard data formats for graphics files on the Macintosh: EPSF (Encapsulated PostScript), TIFF (Tagged Image File Format), RIFF (Raster Image File Format), and PICT. Not all page layout and illustration programs will allow you to place all of these different kinds of files as illustrations. Your scanner may produce a format that your illustration program doesn't recognize. When buying your system make sure that your scanner, illustration program, and page layout software speak the same dialect. Most Macintosh programs recognize PICT files, many also support TIFF, and a good many programs understand EPSF, too.

*Printing:* If your files won't print, your first step should be to check the connectors in your AppleTalk network ( the cable that runs from the back of the Macintosh to the printer). Especially if you have more than one machine on the network, connectors will work themselves loose. Tighten everything and try again. The Macintosh has a software utility called the Chooser that lets you tell the computer what printer(s) it's currently connected to. If, after tightening the cables, you still get a "printer not found" message, verify that you've selected a printer in the Chooser utility. The manual that comes with your printer should cover this procedure in detail. If not, the Macintosh Utilities Guide you get with the computer does.

Files that won't print properly at your service bureau can usually be traced to one of just three causes. If the file prints, but the wrong fonts appear in the output, there is a font conflict (see page 126).

As developers revise software, sometimes files created with newer revisions can't be opened or printed properly with an older version of the software. If the service bureau's Illustrator® program won't open your Illustrator file, check the version numbers on your program and their program.

If the output is reversed (white on black), mirror-image, or not the size you expected, check the settings in the "Print" dialog box. When you issue a "Print" command, most Macintosh programs present you with a standard dialog box that asks if you want the output reduced or enlarged, positive or negative, with or without crop marks, and so on. Turning on the "enlarged printing area" option in the print dialog box may cause a PostScript error on laser printers if you've used graphics and more than three different fonts in the document.

## Viral Infection

It's a sad fact that not everyone who uses graphics computers does so to enrich the lives of their fellow human beings. There are programmers who create programs designed to get into your data and disrupt it. The disruptions range from inconveniences to the destruction of all the data on your hard disk. When that data is the sum total of your business—project files, client lists, accounting records—it can be devastating.

These destructive programs come in several varieties, but they are generically called "viruses." Some wipe out data. Some freeze the system, refusing to allow you to control your computer. Some just slow processing down to a crawl. They're all dangerous.

## Viral Infections: Causes, Cures

### Avoidance Theory

Putting your computers into a "quarantine" and strictly controlling what goes into them is the first line of defense. Viruses are generally spread when you insert a disk that's been infected with a virus program into your computer. The virus copies itself to your hard disk, and every floppy you use thereafter may have the virus on it as well. Also, if you accept files from other computers via modem, there's a chance those files could be infected.

If you don't use floppy disks that have been in other computers and don't take files via modem, you'll eliminate most of your risk.

A complete quarantine is hard to achieve. Short of isolating your computer, you can take other steps. Buy and use one or two commercial anti-virus programs such as Virex® or SAM® Intercept. SAM can be set up so that each disk that goes into your computer is scanned for viruses before it's read into memory. The caveat is that SAM can only intercept a virus if it knows what it's looking for; a specific piece of code or a suspicious action by the software. To circumvent these precautions, new virus strains are invented monthly, with the virus-makers locked in a twisted game of chess with anti-virus programmers. Unfortunately, we're the pawns. Users are the ones who suffer most when the virus programmers find a way to checkmate the good guys. The commercial programs are upgraded regularly. As a registered user, you'll receive the new versions as they are shipped.

### Keeping A Low Profile

Your risk is related to how and where you exchange data. Users groups are often software swap-meets, with members copying and distributing data profligately. Remember when your mother told you not to put a penny in your mouth because "you don't know where it's been"? Don't put a disk in your computer if you don't know where it's been.

Service bureaus may handle disks from hundreds of users. Some viruses are built so that the effects aren't noticed for days or weeks, so it's hard for a bureau to know immediately when it's been infected. In the meantime, the disks of dozens of users may be infected and returned. Good service bureaus disinfect and check for viruses constantly—ask yours about their anti-virus procedure. If they say, "What procedure?" find a new service bureau.

Colleges and universities are prime sites for epidemics. If you live near a college, the area service bureaus will probably be exposed to disks from the school. If you use a rental machine at a copy center near a college, be cautious. Check any disks run in their machines with your anti-virus programs.

If your machines begin slowing down inexplicably, if you begin experiencing system crashes more frequently, or if you begin losing data files, suspect a virus. If you don't have the latest bug-sniffers, get them. Check the hard disks in all of your machines, then check floppies you've used recently. Ask around. Find out if a virus has turned up in your area recently, what its symptoms are, and how to cure it.

If the problems continue, take your disks to a dealer and have them checked. Tell the technician that you suspect a virus so he doesn't infect other machines. If a virus is confirmed, ask for help in removing it. Some viruses can be "snipped" from healthy data files using ResEdit, an Apple utility. Don't try this unless you know what you're doing as you could permanently cripple the files. If this doesn't work, you may have to reformat the hard disk. Unfortunately, this will also wipe out your data. You may be able to replace some files from your backup archive, but archives made while your machines were infected may well be infected themselves.

# *Chapter Fourteen:*
# *Business Class*

**Business Class:**
**Software For A Smart Studio**

**Estimating, Tracking, Accounting**

**Studio/Soft:**
**Dreams For Design Studio Management**

## Business Class: Software For A Smart Studio

uriously, the business applications of computers get scant attention from too many designers. Business functions—accounting, data management, word processing—were the first non-scientific applications for computers. They remain by far the largest area of application for desktop computers. Studios that gladly spend $20,000 to install two or three graphics work stations are slow to take advantage of the tremendous power those work stations offer them to plan, control, and profit from their businesses.

Granted, most design workstations are based on the Apple Macintosh. And business software is one area in which the IBM compatible computers have a clear advantage over Apple. The reasons are simple. The installed base of IBM users is huge, making development of business software for IBM compatible machines less risky. Developers were creating business software for IBMs for years before the Macintosh was created. The number of third-party developers of IBM compatible software dwarfs the number of Macintosh developers. And until 1987, the Macintosh didn't have the raw computing power needed to cut it in the world of relational database management—the type of software that's at the heart of many integrated business applications. Add the natural advantages posed by the easy communications link between IBM compatible desktop computers and IBM mainframe computers, and you have a shut-out.

More Macs are finding their way into the business world—analysts estimated that about a tenth of Apple's production in 1989 was sold to large corporations—but it will be some time before they're a common sight in corporate accounting offices.

In many businesses, "integrated applications" have been the norm for a decade or more. In a manufacturing company, for example, this might mean that the sales department's contract data is linked to the purchasing department, so that materials needed to fulfill new contracts is ordered in time to meet the delivery date. The integration extends to accounting—which gets sales data from the sales department and delivery information from the shipping department—and to management, marketing, and even down onto the factory floor, where workers log hours spent on each job into a terminal or use computers to control machinery.

This kind of door-to-door integration is unusual in the design business.

Larger studios tended to have IBM compatible machines in place to handle their business management needs before buying Macintosh stations for the designers. Many smaller studios, with fewer clients and lower revenues, get by with paper-based accounting systems.

Lack of precedent is no reason not to take advantage of the Macintosh business software, much of it quite good, that does exist. It's possible to set up an integrated management system using Macintosh computers. Also, in this age of connectivity, it's easy enough to network the IBM compatible computers used for "front of house" activities—accounting and management—with Macintosh stations in the studio (see *Studio/Soft: Dreams For Design Studio Management*, page 146).

Until truly integrated software is available for design studios, you'll have to make do with a piecemeal approach to computerizing your business functions. Despite the limitations, the benefits are enormous.

### Pricing

Graphics computers can make your studio more efficient, allowing you to pocket the savings or pass them on to your clients. Designers caution against price-cutting. You may well be able to cut prices after adding a graphics computer, but

## PAT DAVIS DESIGN: Under Control

*Pat Davis*
*Pat Davis Design*
*Founded 1980*
*Five designers*
*Graphics computer equipment: four Macintosh SE and SE30 CPUs, 19-inch monitors, extended keyboards, Apple Laserwriter printer, internal hard disk drives*

An early convert to the Macintosh way, the Sacramento studio of Pat Davis is now in its third year of fully digital production.

"We do a lot of work for Intel, Hewlett-Packard, and other computer manufacturers. They almost require that we have desktop publishing," Pat Davis explained. "I don't think about the cost of the equipment anymore; I think about what it would have cost if we had lost those clients or not gotten them."

Davis has gone beyond illustration, paste-up, and output, however. The Macintosh has become a tool not only for design, but for the management of her studio as well. DesignSoft® software allows Davis to track the actual time spent against her estimates for every job the studio does.

The designers turn in time sheets each day to the production manager. The manager enters the time spent by each designer into the program. The program automatically totals the hours spent by project and makes a report, available on disk or paper, of estimated time against actual time for each project.

The software also allows Davis to track the billable hours generated by each designer.

"When a designer comes to me to talk about salary, I can find out very quickly how they're doing. If they're not generating revenue for the studio, I can show them where they need to improve," Davis explained.

The ability to track time spent for each project against the job estimates has helped Davis work with clients more effectively, too.

"If we have a client we're not making a profit on because their work takes more time, I can negotiate a higher rate," she said.

How does it go over? "So far, no one has turned me down. They can see for themselves that their work takes more time."

Davis said the studio sells quality design and that the clients understand good design takes time. She has not used the computer equipment as a means to cut prices, but has noticed other positive economic benefits.

"With DesignSoft, I can see that the computers have helped make the designers better profit centers," she explained.

Good equipment is part of the equation. When the studio moved into its current quarters, which occupy 3,000 square feet, Davis planned the computers in from the start. Custom U-shaped work stations keep each designer's area organized. The computers are kept to one side of the station while a drafting board occupies the other.

While DesignSoft and the work stations keep the studio running smoothly on the inside, Davis said the computers have had a tremendous impact on client relationships too.

"We can show much better comps using the computers," she said. "Better comps take the mystery out of the design process. The clients trust us more and trust us quicker. That makes them more receptive to our work."

can you sell enough more work to make up for a drop in total revenues? If you now sell ten jobs at $10,000 each, having a graphics computer might allow you to sell those jobs for $7,500 each. If you cut prices, however, your total revenues will drop from $100,000 to $75,000. Depending on your profit margin, you might have to sell two or three additional $7,500 jobs to earn as much profit as you did before you added the computers. If you've already absorbed all of the work available to you, you may find yourself losing, rather than gaining, profits.

While a few designers choose to cut prices to attract more business, the vast majority use the savings to bolster their bottom line. In fact, it's not uncommon for studio owners to levy a surcharge for work that's done on a computer.

## Estimating

At the very least, buy a spreadsheet program such as Microsoft Excel® or Informix WingZ®. With very little effort, you can create a form that will automate your estimates. A spreadsheet provides a way to answer questions such as "What if we have to hire a freelancer to complete the job on schedule?" or "What if the client rejects two designs and we have to do a third—or even fourth—round of comps?"

While these questions can be answered with a calculator and a piece of paper, the spreadsheet will do it faster and it never makes mistakes in addition. Also, because your type will be priced per finished page rather than per galley, and your corrections should be minimal, your estimates will likely be more accurate. In our own estimate sheet, we figure that 10 percent of the pages will be set twice. To date, that's been a reliable guide and can serve as a starting point for you.

Especially for pricing large or repetitive projects, the spreadsheet will allow you to give quotes faster and more accurately.

## Tracking

For those large or complex projects, a computer can be an invaluable tracking tool. Using a database program or spreadsheet, you can keep tabs on the innumerable small details.

Two years ago, we designed and produced the mechanicals for a book that contained 450 four-color ads and approximately 1,000 color transparencies. Each ad came from a different client, was sold by one of a half-dozen salespeople, and had an individual layout and copy. The materials had to be logged as they arrived, tardy advertisers reminded to send their copy and transparencies, the ads had to designed, and laser proofs sent and returned with signatures.

In less than an hour, we created a database form that provided space for the name, address, and telephone number of each client, boxes to tell us when their materials were due, whether they were in or not, whether they had been designed or not, whether a proof had been sent and, if so, when it was due back, and whether a mechanical had been shipped to the printer.

By simply filling in copies of this form on the computer, we were able to quickly tell how we were doing on the project. The database program allowed us to print reports showing whose material was overdue, which ads were in and needed to be designed, and who needed to get proofs back to us.

Spreadsheets are a good way to keep track of materials sent to clients or printers. We use a five column spreadsheet to track our book projects. Column one lists the page numbers. Column two shows whether each page has been sent to the printer. Columns three through five show the number of transparencies (35mm, 2 ¼ or 6x7, and 4x5) for each page. The columns are tabulated at the top of the spreadsheet. By simply looking at the top of the sheet, we can tell at a glance how many pages have been shipped and how many transparencies of what sizes have been sent. This makes it faster to write transmittals and the spreadsheet is usually more accurate than doing a count by hand.

### Billing/Accounting

Your clients can't pay you for your time if you don't keep track of it and bill it properly. A low-tech solution is to use a spreadsheet program to create time logs for each designer. Rows one through thirty-one can be the days of the month while each column represents a different project. If you can get designers to log their time on these sheets, it will be easy enough for you to pick the sheets up on disk each week and link them so that all hours for each client are automatically added together.

An integrated software package such as DesignSoft (see *Pat Davis Design*, page 143) will do this for you automatically.

The number of excellent billing and accounting programs available for IBM and compatible computers is mind boggling. In addition, programmers who create custom applications from basic database programs, such as Dbase IV®, can create a billing and accounting package just for you. If you have an IBM computer in your studio, this is a good use for it.

There are several full-featured accounting programs that run on Macintosh computers and more will undoubtedly appear by the time you read this. These programs go far beyond the basics of bill this and pay that. They are sophisticated, multi-module programs capable of handling businesses with revenues up to $5 million. If you have some familiarity with accounting, it's possible to set up the ledgers, disbursement journals, and so on yourself. If not, you may be able to get an accountant to help you. Either way, someone in the studio will have to be in charge of entering bills as they come in and logging checks as they're written out.

The advantages of keeping your books on your own computer are that you have instant access to your financial profile, can instantly forecast cash flow, and can keep close tabs on how much you're paying vendors and employees. Expenses that tend to balloon unnoticed, such as air express bills, telephone, and office supplies can be monitored weekly or monthly and excesses quickly checked.

A disadvantage to this system is that you may find it distracts you from designing, that you keep the books improperly, or that the information in the file can be read or erased by a mischievous associate. If you keep financial data on your computer, buy and use a security program. These allow you to lock sensitive files. A password is required before they can be reopened. Some programs even keep a log, posting an entry every time someone tries to access a locked file. Security is especially important if your computers are networked together.

### Marketing/Productivity

Your computer should be used to help you market yourself more effectively. This can be done by keeping a database of clients. Each time you talk to someone, log it in a database and key in a follow-up date. Each week, run a report showing who you should follow up with, their phone number, and the subject of your last conversation. It's possible, using Smart Alarms® or another utility, to have your computer sound an alarm when it's time to make a phone call or prepare for a meeting. These alarms can be scheduled up to a year in advance, and scheduled activities can be viewed by the day, week, or month. Focal Point® is another such program, as is C.A.T.® They can keep your marketing responsibilities organized, and your attention can remain focused on design without letting sales and follow-up slide.

## ROLL YOUR OWN: Charting Features For A Complete Management Information System

So far, the ultimate customizable door-to-door information management system for design studios hasn't appeared. It may be in development. It may be available by the time you read this. But right now, the dream of a single software package that seamlessly integrates all business and production functions is still that—a dream. Some excellent beginnings exist, in AdMan and DesignSoft.

What's required is a software system modeled on the full-featured accounting packages that allows you to buy modules—one for time and billing, another for scheduling and tracking, another for

accounting—to build a system with as much or as little power as you need.

Designers should be able to log their times and enter purchase orders on-line, so that no re-typing is needed later. For managers, the project sheets should print daily schedules with an alarms feature (a note appears one week before a project milestone, for example) and all the reports should be available to managers on-line instantaneously. Purchase orders entered for clients with overdue balances should automatically "freeze" in the system so a case-by-case review can be made.

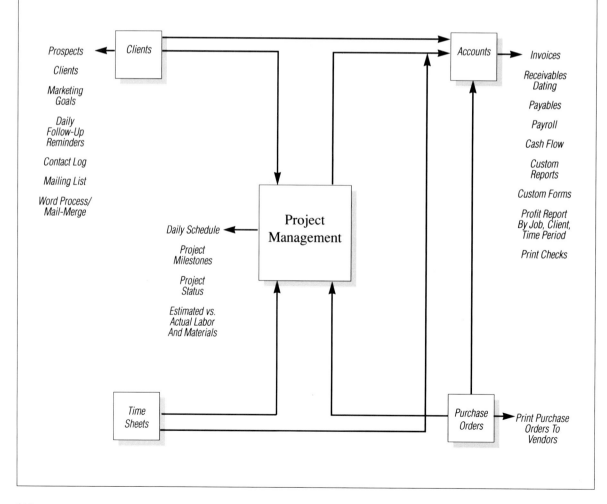

# Chapter Fifteen:
# Heading For A Far Horizon

**Changing Times**

At the beginning of this book we talked about whether you should add graphics computers to your studio. By now, you've probably already made the decision to do so. Hopefully, you've also realized that, while computers are just another tool, their abilities touch so many facets of the design studio that they can create an alternative way of approaching, planning, and conducting your business.

Installing a functioning graphics computer system is just the first step down that alternative road. Where it will ultimately lead is an open question, as the technology is changing rapidly.

Given the enormous cost advantages gained by using graphics computers and the design edge they can give you, it's hard for us not to believe that digital design will be the norm in the very near future, and that studios that use *only* traditional methods will be in the minority.

While many studios make the decision to buy a graphics computer because they want to be able to set their own type, after they've used it for six months, they no longer see that as the most important benefit. Instead, they tend to talk about time, manpower, and the "next step."

### The Time Line

Aside from being a wonderful tool for visualization, a graphics computer makes it possible to spend more time designing projects and less time executing them.

"I don't think of the computer as just saving dollars," reflected Mark Crumpacker. "You don't want to make yourself so efficient that you're just cranking out work quickly. I think of the computer as allowing more time for design. Not only do you get a better end product from a technical point of view, but you can get a better *design* because the computer relieves you of the most time-consuming aspects of actually making the end product."

*In order to "capture" that time, however, you have to make an effort to adjust your process.* First, don't throw away your sketch pad altogether, but do *get the work into the computer as early in the process as possible*; hopefully just after the thumbnail stage. Second, *every time you sit down at the monitor, think about the end product*, the electronic file that will be sent to a service bureau. Third, *merge together as many steps as you can.* When making a rough from a thumbnail, take the time to place the page margins, type, and graphics accurately instead of just eyeballing them. Later, when you clean up the rough to make the comp, you'll have less work to do and there won't be any surprises (like a photo that doesn't crop into a tight space). When you make the comp, again think end product. Clean up the file so that, when the client approves the design, you don't spend half a day finding the inaccuracies in the file and repairing them. If you begin a file with the idea that, at any time, it could be made ready for the service bureau with little effort, you'll find new ways to take steps out of your process.

*Whenever possible, solve whole problems rather than parts of problems.* Creating half of a design and thinking, "We'll work out the rest of it later," will increase the number of hours you spend on a project. It takes almost as much time to do something inaccurately as it does to do it accurately. One of the most striking things we've noticed about designers who use computers is that their approach to design becomes more comprehensive. They look at their projects as a whole and try to solve them as a whole, rather than building a solution from a collection of individual parts.

This discipline is partly the result of the nature of the computer as a tool; just operating it requires a somewhat organized thought process. The computer also encourages whole-pie solutions because you're able to see—on the screen, in living color—all of the pieces of even a complex project. They can be printed out in the studio with real type and real images in place and the prints arranged side by side for evaluation.

## Multiplying Manpower

A graphics computer alters the traditional concept of manpower for a studio. *The quality of a studio's computer skills become as important as the quantity of board artists.*

Good computer skills can help make up for the lack of a staff illustrator by allowing you to substitute photo-illustrations or scanned art for conventional renderings. And they can make up for deficiencies in paste-up, too. Few board artists can place type and images with an accuracy of $1/1000$ of an inch, but the computer does so as a matter of course.

For smaller studios, a graphics computer can help more effectively handle the varied tasks required to keep the studio running. As a business partner, the computer can keep track of vital marketing information and even remind you when it's time to make a phone call to secure a new project. It can track the time spent on current projects and compare it to the hours budgeted. It can watch the progress of the work, warn when deadlines are approaching, and even compare the relative efficiency of designers.

All of these things can be done without computers, of course, but you can do them faster and with less effort using a computer, making it more likely you'll attempt them.

The powerful production capabilities of the computer can have an effect, too. By reducing the number of man-hours required to produce both good comps and final mechanicals, it allows studios to take on more extensive projects than they could reasonably complete using conventional methods. The computer solves the problem of whether to hire more designers in order to take on big projects, or whether to get the projects and then scramble to find the people to complete them. Bigger projects can mean bigger revenues, bigger clients, and bigger creative opportunities.

## The Next Step

Few designers who convert to digital design remain satisfied with the basics—typesetting and paste-up—for very long. Once they've tasted the flexibility and freedom to experiment offered by graphics computers, their minds begin churning, conceiving new ways to apply the computer's abilities to their craft. Inevitably, they dream of even more sophisticated hardware and software for more sophisticated solutions. What seems fast and high-tech in the beginning quickly becomes routine. They're constantly yearning for that "next step" in the evolution of the tools.

Just a few short years ago, the frontier of graphics applications was easy to see and reach. You could make mechanicals, set type, and produce crude (by today's standards) illustrations. Today, the frontier has moved on, to designing in full color and producing plate-ready four-color negatives directly from the desktop; to building animation sequences and three-dimensional images for output to video; to sound editing and creating hypermedia. These applications were wishful thinking eighteen months ago. Today they're reality.

Making predictions is always risky, but there are too many exciting developments that appear to be just over the horizon for us to resist.

Telecommunications will play a larger role in design studios. With a graphics computer and a modem, you can be connected to a network of freelancers whose drawing tables are literally as close as the telephone. Their sketches can be on your screen in minutes; finished files in your layouts in hours. The facsimile and telephone will never replace face-to-face working relationships, but as the AT&T ads say, telecommunication *is* the next best thing to being there.

While we may be a long way from the day when geography is conquered by telecommunications, its importance has been diminished. We're old enough to remember roaming through Manhattan combing the files at the photo houses —Magnum, Black Star, Image Bank—in search of the perfect stock photo. In 1990, Image Bank will make its catalog of images available via modem. Dial-up, keyword searches will become a reality for designers from Durango to Durham. Typing in "tiger" will bring up pictures of both the Siberian and Detroit varieties. When you find what you want, press a button and you have a color photograph on your hard disk, ready to drop into a layout. Another hour and you're ready to transmit the completed page to a service bureau for film separations. The next day, you're looking at a color proof.

The price of quality digital color printing devices will drop. This could open up a new market for studios in creating and producing short-run color documents. While production-grade equipment capable of quickly churning out a hundred copies of an eight-page document will probably remain too expensive for most studios to own, the printers will be available at service bureaus, much as imagesetters are today. Devices capable of shorter runs should be affordable even for smaller studios.

Creating plate-ready composite four-color film with photographic separations in place will become a frequent—if not everyday—practice. Initially, the equipment to do this will be located at the service bureaus, who will help with the technical aspects of separating the photographs. As the power of the software increases, the amount of skill needed by the operator will drop, as will prices on the hardware, opening the way for this function to move from the service

bureau to the studio. It's likely that the equipment to actually image the film will stay in the service bureaus.

Rendering designs in three dimensions in software will become common, and the high-quality three-dimensional images now associated with ray tracing and other exotic imaging techniques will also become commonplace.

Some designers will get into creating "virtual realities." A virtual reality is a world created inside of a computer and is the perfect medium for training simulations and for architectural and interior design. By wearing special goggles containing a color display, a viewer can be immersed in this "reality" and, with special equipment, can even enter and interact with it.

The raw computing power required for these applications will be supplied by super-powerful desktop computers. Some of them will be based on RISC technology, which distributes tasks to a series of chips, rather than making one chip do all the work.

### Full Circle
We've come back to the point where we started —with Lance Hidy's prediction that computers will have as dramatic an effect on the graphic arts as did the invention of movable type.

You have to decide whether you want to participate in this change and to what extent. Computer graphics hardware and software were easier to grasp and learn four years ago than they are today. Every new software program upgrade adds features, and new features add complexity. The longer you wait to jump, the harder the leap will be. You'll have more to learn, more history to catch up on. Deciding whether and when to join the party is probably the most critical career choice you'll make in the next five years. Reading this book was the first step. We hope it's been a useful one.

# Chapter Sixteen:
# Reference And Resources

**What Is PostScript?**

**Color From The Desktop**

**Rasters And Resolution**

**Resource Listings**

**Index**

# What Is PostScript?

Whenever there's a discussion about desktop publishing, the term Post-Script® seems to come up. There's a good reason for that. In large measure, PostScript made desktop publishing possible.

PostScript is the name of a page description language created and marketed by Adobe Systems, which also developed the popular Adobe Illustrator® drawing software.

## Page Description Languages

A page description language is a computer program that tells printing devices—such as photo-typesetters, laser printers, or impact printers—where to place dots on a piece of paper or film to form an image. Aside from using pre-defined shapes (such as a photographic negative of an alphabet or the metal type element of a typewriter) there are two basic models for doing this. One is called bit-mapping. The other is called vector imaging.

Bit-map page description languages hold in memory a "map" that breaks down a piece of paper into a finite number of dots or pixels (picture elements). These dots can be turned "on" (to print black or some other color) or "off" (no printing). In order to properly map the paper, the software has to know how many dots there are on the page. This will depend on the resolution of the printing device being used. The more dots a printer places per square inch, the higher its resolution and the smoother the images printed with it will appear. A twenty-four pin dot-matrix computer printer places more dots in each square inch than one with only twelve pins. A laser printer places more dots per square inch than a twenty-four pin printer. And an imagesetter places many more dots than a laser printer. In order to place dots using any of these printers, a bit-map program has to know the location of each dot on the page. Therefore, the program has to know in advance what kind of printer will be used and what its resolution is.

A designer working in a software program that uses a bit-map language is limited to working in a single resolution. If the object is to create reproduction-quality materials, resolution should be greater than 1,000 dots per linear inch (1 million dots per square inch). Until recently, computer printers capable of that degree of resolution cost more than $35,000 .

Not many studios have been willing to invest that much money in on-site imaging equipment. Also, once the size of a bit-mapped object is set, it can't be changed without degrading the image. The stem of the letter "r" in eight-point Helvetica, for example, might be four pixels wide. When you enlarge a bit-map, the printer prints the same number of pixels. The individual pixels just get bigger to cover the larger print area, making the image "grainy." Enlarging the eight-point "r" to twenty points would spread the pixels over a larger area, and you'd see a stair-step effect in the curves. In a bit-map language, the computer needs an individual bit map for each size and style of type that will be used.

PostScript is not a bit-map language. It uses vector imaging. Instead of mapping the precise location of each dot on a page, it describes images as a series of outlines, called vectors.

Vectors are sort of like a connect-the-dot puzzle. If you enlarge a connect-the-dot puzzle on a photocopier, the dots will be farther apart, but the *outline* of the object the dots define will remain the same. The object just gets bigger. A vector language defines what appears inside of the outline by specifying the space within outlines as "fills." A fill can be another vector image, a color, a dot screen, even a gradated tint. When you enlarge a vector image, the outline and the fill cover a larger area, but the individual pixels remain the same size. The printer prints more of them to cover the larger area. You no longer need a separate font for each size and style of type. Instead, the outline for one font can be scaled up or down as needed.

This ability to see the page as outlines and fills, rather than individual dots with specific spatial locations, makes PostScript and other vector languages "device independent." Unlike a bit-map language, they don't need to know in advance the number of individual pixels a printing device is able to put on a piece of paper. Files created and proofed on a low-resolution (and low-cost) laser printer can also be printed on a high-resolution imagesetter. In each case, PostScript prints the image at the maximum resolution the printer is capable of. The $35,000-plus piece of equipment can stay at the typesetter's office while you do your proofing on a $3,500 device.

## Alternatives And Outlook

PostScript became a standard in the graphics community among both designers and suppliers because it is a common language that computer devices of varying costs and capabilities can use to create reproduction-quality art. Also, it was the output language adopted by Apple Computer for the Macintosh. Together, PostScript and Macintosh created a chain that linked relatively inexpensive desktop computers with high-resolution printers. It has been possible to set type from desktop computers since the late 1970s, but, until the release of the Macintosh, doing so required learning and using arcane commands enclosed in brackets to specify type styles, sizes, and positioning. With a desktop computer and a PostScript printer, designers can see type and images on their computer screen more or less as they will appear when printed. This was the real breakthrough, the one called "WYSIWYG," or "whizzywig." WYSIWYG stands for "What you see is what you get."

In reality, what you see is not always what you get. Neither the Macintosh nor IBM compatibles use PostScript for screen display. The Macintosh screen display is created in a language called QuickDraw. The two languages draw images differently. Occasionally, therefore, what you see on the screen won't match what comes out of the printer.

The NeXT® computer built by ex-Apple Computer president Steve Jobs uses PostScript for both output and screen display. Apple itself has stayed away from PostScript as a display language in part because its owner, Adobe, has charged premium prices to license the language.

PostScript is far from perfect, however. For one thing, it's slow. When printing complex pages, pages with many fonts, or detailed illustrations on a high-resolution imagesetter, PostScript's imaging process can eat up enormous chunks of RAM and take half an hour or more to print. Print times of ten hours for one set of four-color separations are not unheard of. PostScript has trouble handling some four-color screens, and moiré patterns can appear in separations made from a PostScript file.

In 1989, Apple and Microsoft announced that they would release a competing technology they called Royal. The language would be available on both IBM compatible computers (as is PostScript) and the Apple Macintosh line. Reportedly, Royal font files could be shared by IBM compatible and Macintosh computers.

Whether Royal actually goes into production and whether its advantages are clear enough to win over the huge base of PostScript users has yet to be seen. Given the enormous investment the graphic arts community already has in PostScript devices and fonts, those advantages would have to be tremendous. As one service bureau owner put it, "It's going to take a lot longer to get away from PostScript than it took to adopt it."

## Color From The Desktop

By the time you read this, the era of creating and separating continuous-tone color images—once the exclusive domain of minicomputer-based work stations—will be fully upon us. Page layouts containing type and color photographic images can be assembled on a desktop computer and magazine-quality separations printed from them using one of several methods.

Since the Macintosh was released in 1984, publishers have dreamed of being able to use relatively inexpensive desktop computers to generate composite color film for offset printing. This eliminates the need for mechanical boards, color separation houses, random proofs, and manual stripping. It completely merges the processes of design and production, bringing them in-house where they can be controlled more easily. It cuts days, or even weeks, off of the time needed to take a project from page design to putting it on a press.

The link established between page layout files created in Quark XPress® and the Scitex Visionary® system in 1989 was the first (sort of) direct-from-desktop high-quality color system. We say "sort of" because the Macintosh is used to create type, position, size, and crop the photographs, but expensive Scitex equipment is required to scan the four-color art and output the color separations. The results are spectacular. The separations are as good as "conventional" separations because they are just that—created on conventional, high-end color equipment.

As of this writing, we've not been able to find an economic justification for using such a system. Presently, color prep houses using the Visionary system are charging $175 to $350 per letter-sized page for composite film. Even at that price, the composite film still has to be stripped into signatures by the printer. Comparable separations can be made conventionally and stripped up by hand for less money.

Other proprietary systems have appeared. One of these, CyberChrome®, is based on desktop CPUs, but uses a high-end scanner to input the color images. The Macintosh, again, is used only to position and crop photos and image type. The prices we were quoted for composite film created on the CyberChrome system were as much or more than it cost to produce the same materials at a conventional prep house.

A variety of color scanners have been introduced for use with desktop graphics computers. One of the most popular to date has been the Sharp JX-450, a flatbed scanner with an optional accessory that allows it to scan transparencies as well as reflective art.

As this book was going to press, Nikon released a scanner for 35mm transparencies, the LS-3500. While not the first 35mm scanner on the market, the results shown by the designers and pre-press houses privileged to have used the machine at the time of publication are very exciting. We saw a nine-inch by twelve-inch separation made from a 35mm slide that was better than many conventional separations we've had made. The color image on page sixteen was reproduced from a piece created entirely from slides scanned with the LS-3500.

When teamed up with Adobe PhotoShop® or Letraset ColorStudio® software, the LS-3500 can produce magazine-quality separations that can be printed directly to film from a desktop computer. At the time of its introduction, the LS-3500 was priced at $10,000.

The files created by any color scanner and separation software package are enormous. When run at full resolution the LS-3500 reportedly produces files as large as 75 mb for one four-color image. Storing and moving that data is as critical as creating it. If you plan to get into making separations, plan to spend some cash for several high-capacity disks (either optical or Winchester). If you're considering transferring this data between computers, you'll need an Ethernet connection to handle the files without bringing your network to its knees.

One problem that has plagued early users of direct-from-desktop color separations is the crudeness of PostScript's halftoning compared to the sophisticated imaging models used in high-end separation equipment such as the Scitex.

When making four-color separations, separators rotate the dot screen of each of the four pieces of film (those used to print cyan, magenta, yellow, and black), offsetting them from each other. If the angles used to make these offsets are incorrect, moiré patterns can result. Typical rotation values for the screens are 105 degrees off vertical for cyan, 75 degrees for magenta, 90 degrees for yellow, and 45 degrees for black.

PostScript, however, is not capable of producing every possible combination of screen angle and screen density. When a PostScript device receives a command from a software package to set an angle/density combination that it doesn't support, it automatically substitutes another value for the angle. This can lead to some surprising results.

Adobe has been aware of this problem for some time, and a new version of PostScript optimized for color work has been announced for release in the second half of 1990.


### Desktop Printers

While graphic artists often have to think in terms of putting color on paper with a printing press, there are many new applications for color computer printers.

Producing comps is obviously one, but others—such as preparing business presentation materials and even creating reproduction art for a conventional separator—are gaining in popularity as the quality of the color available from desktop printing devices increases.

Three of the means computer printers use to print color are thermal wax, inkjet, and dye sublimation.

Thermal wax printers use four ribbons (one for each of the process colors) impregnated with wax-based inks. Heat is used to transfer the wax from the ribbons to a sheet of paper. Their resolution is generally 300 dpi, and in 1990, prices for thermal wax printers ranged from $5,000 to more than $20,000. The more expensive models include PostScript raster image processors that allow full-resolution printing of PostScript outline fonts. Non-PostScript models sometimes substitute crude bit-mapped fonts in their output.

Inkjet printers create color images by spraying colored inks onto the paper. They tend to cost less than thermal wax or sublimal dye printers (between $1,500 and $3,000 at the time of publication) but their color range and resolution are also more limited.

Sublimal dye printers seem to hold the most promise. Ink contained in a ribbon is heated in the printer, turning it to a vapor. The vapor diffuses into a receiving sheet and "sticks" only in the image areas. Unlike thermal wax pigments, the inks can be laid down on top of each other. That increases the apparent sharpness of sublimal dye prints and the smoothness of their color gradations.

The first desktop sublimal dye printers began shipping in late 1989, though their price ($14,000 and up) put them at the high end of the printer range. The Kodak XL7700 produces an eleven inch by eleven inch print that looks much like a conventional photograph. Though it wasn't shipping as this book was going to press, the price had been set at $25,000.

Very expensive sublimal dye printers are used as digital proofing printers by color separators. The Iris 3024 and the DuPont 4Cast (both $75,000 at 1990 prices) are two. See page 26 for an example of a 4Cast sublimal dye print.

## Rasters And Resolution: Color Monitors

It's logical enough to think that a monitor is a monitor is a monitor. Nothing could be further from the truth. Even in what should be a simple matter, the manufacturers seem to have conspired to make buying a monitor a confusing and arduous undertaking.

First, some terms. "Raster" was originally used to refer to the rows of phosphorescent dots on a television screen that are energized to form a photographic image on the tube. The meaning has expanded to embrace any image made up of dots. In the context of monitors, "resolution" refers not only to number of dots per inch the monitor is capable of displaying, but also to the total size of the image that can be displayed as measured in pixels.

The monitors built into the Macintosh Plus and SE display an image 640 pixels wide by 480 pixels high at a density of 72 dots per inch on a nine-inch screen. IBM VGA graphics displays are also 640 pixels by 480 pixels, but they spread that over a twelve-inch screen.

The resolution of a computer's monitor depends in part on the software being used and in part on the display card used to generate the video signals for the monitor. Most Macintosh software automatically adjusts to take advantage of larger monitors. IBM software does not.

Larger monitors commonly display images that measure 1024 pixels by 768 pixels. The image area shown includes most of two letter-sized pages viewed side by side. Some sixteen-inch monitors display 1024 pixels by 808 pixels, resulting in a screen resolution of 82 dpi.

The monitor's density in dots per inch is important because Macintosh software assumes that the monitor is 72 dpi. Screen densities higher or lower than 72 dpi can alter the size of objects displayed on the screen. For example, a box that, when printed, will measure one inch by one inch also measures one inch by one inch when displayed on the screen of a 72 dpi moni-

tor. However, on an 82 dpi monitor (equivalent to 1024 by 808 pixels on a sixteen-inch screen), the box would measure only three-quarters of an inch by three-quarters of an inch. The inconvenience of this mismatch is minor as you won't often be relying on a one-to-one correspondence between screen display size and output size, but it can throw your eye off a bit until you get used to it.

### Two Bits, Four Bits, Eight Bits

When talking about color monitors, you have to be specific about how many colors you want to see on the screen simultaneously. A black and white display maps only one of two colors to each of the screen's pixels: black or white. More colors require more pixels. Eight-bit display cards and monitors allow you to see 256,000 colors on the screen simultaneously. Twenty-four bit and thirty-two bit displays show up to 16.7 million colors on screen. These are "full color" or "photographic color" displays. They are, of course, vastly more expensive than mere eight-bit displays.

You'll want to know how much RAM a color display card includes (the more the better, as video images require a lot of data) and whether there are special features built in. These may include hardware zoom and pan (which allow you to "zoom in" on or "pan across" a screen image without having to wait for a full screen redraw). Some display cards have provisions for importing or exporting NTSC video signals. NTSC is a set of standards that define the electrical characteristics of color signals used by broadcasters. If you plan to use your computer to produce images on videotape, you'll need an NTSC-compatible board. Other display boards offer "frame grabbers" that digitize video signals from a camera or videocassette recorder for use in your files.

# Resources: Names And Numbers

The following list is not all-inclusive, but is offered to give you a place to begin gathering information. Addresses and telephone numbers were current at the time of publication, but they may have changed by the time you read this.

## Publications

*Byte*
One Phoenix Mill Ln., Peterborough, NH 03458
(603) 924-9281 Subscriptions: (800) 257-9402

*Desktop Communications*
48 E. 43rd Street, New York, NY 10017
(212) 867-9650 Subscriptions: (800) 966-9052

*HOW*
1507 Dana Ave., Cincinnati, OH 45207
(513) 531-2222 Subscriptions: (800) 333-1115

*The Macintosh Buyer's Guide*
660 Beachland Blvd., Vero Beach, FL 32693
(407) 231-6904

*Macworld*
501 Second Street, San Francisco, CA 94107
(415) 243-0505 Subscriptions: (800) 525-0643

*MacUser*
950 Tower Lane, Foster City, CA 94404
(415) 378-5600 Subscriptions: (800) 627-2247

*PC Magazine*
One Park Ave., New York, NY 10016
(212) 503-5255 Subscriptions: (800) 627-2247

*Publish!*
501 Second Street, San Francisco, CA 94107
(415) 243-0505 Subscriptions: (800) 525-0643

*Step-By-Step Electronic Design*
6000 N. Forest Park Dr., Peoria, IL 61614
Subscriptions: (800) 255-8800

## Manufacturers/Developers

Adobe Systems, Inc.
1585 Charleston Rd., Mountain View, CA 94039
(415) 961-4400

Agfa Compugraphic Corporation
200 Ballardvale St., Wilmington, MA 01887
(800) 622-8973

Aldus Corporation
411 First Ave., Seattle, WA 98104
(206) 622-5500

Apple Computer Inc.
20525 Mariani Ave., Cupertino, CA 95014
(415) 996-1010

Bitstream, Inc.
215 First St., Cambridge, MA 02142
(800) 522-3668 (617) 497-6222

Broderbund Software
17 Paul Dr., San Rafael, CA 94903
(415) 492-3500

Deneba Systems, Inc.
3305 NW 74th Ave., Miami, FL 33122
(800) 622-6827 (305) 594-6965

DuPont Corporation
(800) 654-4567

IBM Corporation
101 Paragon Dr., Montvale, NJ 07645
(800) 426-2468

Informix Software
16011 College Blvd., Wichita, KS 66129
(800) 438-7627

Letraset USA
40 Eisenhower Dr., Paramus, NJ 07653
(201) 845-6100

## Resources: Names And Numbers

Linotype Co.
425 Oser Ave., Hauppauge, NY 11788
(800) 645-5764  (516) 434-2000

Micrografx, Inc.
1303 Arapaho, Richardson, TX  75081
(800) 272-3729  (214) 234-1769

Microsoft Corp.
16011 NE 36th Way, Redmond, WA 98052
(800) 426-9444

Nikon Electronic Imaging
101 Cleveland Ave., Bayshore, NY 11706
(516) 222-0200

Quark, Inc.
300 S. Jackson, Ste. 100, Denver, CO 80209
(800) 543-7711  (303) 934-2211

Safeware
2929 N. High Street, Columbus, OH 43202
(800) 848-3469 or (614) 262-0559

SuperMac Technology
458 Potrero Ave., Sunnyvale, CA  94086
(408) 245-2202

Xerox Corporation
Desktop Software Div.
9745 Business Park Ave., San Diego, CA 92131
(800) 822-8221

### Electronic Information Systems

CompuServe, Inc.
5000 Arlington Centre Blvd., Columbus, OH 43220
(800) 848-8199

Connect, Inc.
10101 Bubb Rd., Cupertino, CA 95104
(800) 262-2638  (408) 973-0110

### Users Groups

Apple Computer Inc.
20525 Mariani Ave., Cupertino, CA 95014
(415) 996-1010

The Boston Computer Society
One Center Plaza, Boston, MA 02108
(617) 367-8080

### Books

*Adobe Illustrator '88*
by Tony Bove, Fred E. Davis, and Cheryl Rhodes
Bantam Electronic Publishing
(800) 223-6834 ext. 9479

*Desktop Typography With Quark XPress*
by Frank Romano
Windcrest/TAB Books
Blue Ridge Summit, PA 17294

*Excel In Business*
by Douglas Cobb
Microsoft Press
(800) 426-9444

*Postscript Type Sampler*
by Earl Douglas
Mactography
(301) 424-3942

*Quark XPress Tips*
Quark, Inc.
(800) 543-7711  (303) 934-2211

*Using Aldus PageMaker*
by Doug Kramer and Roger Parker
Bantam Electronic Publishing
(800) 223-6834 ext. 9479

*Ventura Publisher*
by Susan Stevens and John Barry
Dow Jones-Irwin
(800) 634-3966  (312) 206-2700

# Index

accelerators 98
Adams, Ansel 76
Adobe Illustrator 16, 43, 44, 52, 56, 84, 85, 99, 102, 122
Adobe PhotoShop 47, 84, 118, 154
Adobe Systems 40
Agfa Compugraphic 126
Aldus FreeHand 43, 44, 56, 85, 86, 99, 102, 118, 122
Aldus PageMaker 40, 43, 77, 83, 99, 118, 127
Apple Computer 38
Apple File Exchange 87
AppleTalk 132, 139
ASCII 42, 50, 87
AT&T 84
audio-visual presentations 48
backing up 133
Bezier curves 52, 122
billing 50
bit maps 152
bit-map graphics 44
bits 35
Bitstream 40
Blount & Walker Visual Communications 119
Borland SideKick 42, 103
Byte magazine 76
bytes 35
Canvas 2 86, 102, 104
CAT 145
CDEVs 138
clock speed 95
color printers 38,155
color separations 154
CompuServe 87, 124
Computer Shopper 118
consultants 74
Corel Draw 85
CPM 83
CPU 34, 84, 89, 94, 95
Cricket Graph 49
Crosfield 43
Crumpacker, Mark 120, 123, 129, 148
CrystalPaint 84
CyberChrome 154
Davis, Pat 122, 136, 143
Dbase 87, 145
DesignSoft 50, 143, 146
desktop 76

Digital Darkroom 84, 86
Digital Equipment VAX 98
display board 38
DOS 83, 86, 87
DuPont 4Cast 129, 155
dye sublimation 38, 155
DynoDex 103
Eastman Kodak 46
EPSF 45, 139
ergonomic furniture 136
Ethernet 132, 155
Excel 48, 87, 144
fax modem 50
file server 132
film recorder 39, 46
Flink, Hans 123
Focal Point 145
font conflicts 126, 134
Fontographer 45
fonts 40
GCC Personal Laser 99
GEnie 87, 124
Glasgow, Dale 117, 129
Graphic Connexions 130
graphical user interface 90
hard disk 39
Hell 43
Hewlett Packard Desk Jet 99
Hidy, Lance 10, 17, 52, 66, 123
Hopkins, Will 56
Hornall Anderson Design Works 116, 123, 136
HOW Magazine 76
Image Bank 150
Image Club Type Vendor 102
imagesetter 38
InBox 132
INITs 138
input devices 36
insurance 110
integrated applications 142
Intel 80386, 80486 95, 97
International Typeface Corporation 40
Iris printer 129
keyboard 34
Kodachrome 46
Kodak XL-7700 155

## Acknowledgements

Many designers and publishers contributed their advice, experiences, and work to this volume. We want to thank them sincerely. Special thanks are due to: Mark Crumpacker, Derek White, Hans Flink, Marc Passarelli, Pat Davis, Jim Davis, Allie Davis, Tom Lewis, Brian O'Neill, Jack Anderson, John Hornall, Jay Williams, Lance Hidy, Rob Day, Dale Glasgow, Juan Thomassie, Klaus Heesch, Nick Lilavois, and Lloyd Schultz. This book would not have been possible without the stout support of the publishing team at North Light Books: Budge Wallis, Mert Ransdell, and David Lewis. Thanks are also due our editors, Diana Martin and Mary Cropper, and the designer, Clare Finney.

MacIntosh is a registered trademark of Apple Computer, Inc. IBM, IBM-PC, and IBM-AT are registered trademarks of IBM Corporation. Other trademarks are the property of their respective owners: Aldus Corp.—Aldus PageMaker and Aldus FreeHand; Adobe Systems, Inc.—Adobe Illustrator, Adobe PhotoShop, PostScript; SuperMac Technology—PixelPaint, Pixel Paint Professional; Corel—Corel Draw; Micrografx, Inc.—Micrografx Designer; Informix—WingZ; Microsoft Corp.—MS-DOS, Works, Word, Excel; CyberChrome, Inc.—CyberChrome; Scitex America—Scitex, Scitex Visionary; Ashton-Tate—Dbase IV; Eastman Kodak—Kodachrome; General Electric—GEnie; CompuServe, Inc.—CompuServe; MCI Communications—MCI Mail; Deneba Systems, Inc.—UltraPaint, Canvas; Quark, Inc.—Quark XPress; Xerox Corp.—Ventura Publisher; Digital Equipment Corp.—VAX; Cricket Software—Cricket Graph; DuPont Corp.—4Cast; Borland, Intl.—SideKick; Silicon Beach Software—Digital Darkroom; Broderbund Software—TypeStyler; Pantone, Inc.—Pantone, PMS; Letraset USA—Letraset, LetraStudio, PhotoStudio; Altsys Corp.—Fontographer; MicroPro, Inc.—WordStar.

# Index

Landor Associates 120, 123
leases 108
Letraset 40
Letraset ColorStudio 47, 154
LetraStudio 45, 86
Lewis, Tom 62
Linotronic 100, 300 100, 118, 126
Lotus 1-2-3 48, 87
Lumena 84
Macintosh CPUs 95, 97
MacroMind Director 86
MacDraw II 104
MacUser 76, 118
MacVision digitizer 101
MacWeek 47, 76, 118, 133
MacWorld 76
MacWrite 42
mail order 80
maintenance 133
Master Juggler 103, 127
MCI Mail 50, 87
Micrografx Designer 85
Microsoft 38, 83, 84, 90, 100, 153
Microsoft Word 42, 87
Microsoft Works 49
Mink Brook Editions 52
moire patterns 155
Mok, Clement 120
monitor 37, 99, 156
Motorola 6800 95
Motorola 68020, 68030 95
mouse 35
MS-DOS 83, 86, 87
multi-bit displays 156
networks 86, 97, 132
NeXT computer 88, 153
NFNT fonts 127
Nikon LS-3500 154
Nikon scanner 118
NuBus 95
O'Neill, Bryan 116, 123
operating system 83
OPI 43
optical copy recognition 37, 61
OS/2 83, 84, 86
page description languages 152
page layout programs 40
Pantone 42, 66
Palo Alto Research Center 90
Passarelli, Marc 14, 138
PC Computing Magazine 98
PC Magazine 118, 76
PC Week 118
PhotoMac 47, 86
PICT 45, 139
pixel 35, 152
PixelPaint 86, 102
PMS 129
Polaroid 101
PostScript 44, 45, 48, 90, 99, 122, 127, 152, 155
PostScript errors 127, 139
power surges 135
Presentation Manager 90
printer 99
printer resolution 153
PS/2 95

Quantel Paintbox 47, 84
Quark XPress 40, 43, 53, 56, 66, 77, 84, 99, 118, 127, 154
RAM 35
raster image processor 127
Ready Set Go 40
REO drive 39
ResEdit 140
resolution 156
RIFF 45, 139
RIP 127
RISC 88
ROM 35
Royal fonts 100, 153
Safeware Insurance 110
SAM 103, 140
scanner 100
scanners 36
scanning 45
Schultz, Lloyd 82, 118
Scitex 43, 67
Scitex Visionary 130, 154
SCSI 133, 138
service bureaus 126
Smart Alarms 145
SoftPC 87
SpectrePrint 47
spreadsheets 48
Step By Step Electronic Design 76, 124
Stuffit 103
Suitcase II 103, 127
Sun 88
SYLK 87
tablets 36
Targa 84
technologist 132
telecommunications 50
testing imagesetters 129, 130
thirty-two bit CPUs 84
TIFF 45, 139
Timbuktu 132
TimeSlips 50
TOPS 86, 132
tracking/transmittals 144
Trapeze 48, 87
tweening 16
TypeAlign 45
TypeStyler 45
uninterruptible power supply 135
UNIX 89
USA Today 117
used computers 80
utilities 103
VARs 75
vector graphics 44
vector imaging 152
Ventura Publisher 40, 83
VGA graphics 156
Virex 103, 140
virus 139
White, Derek 130
WingZ 48, 87, 144
WordPerfect 42, 87
WordStar 42, 87
WORM 39
WYSIWYG 153
Ziff-Davis Publishing Co. 47, 82, 118